JavaFX Essentials

Create amazing Java GUI applications with this hands-on, fast-paced guide

Mohamed Taman

[PACKT] open source ✿
PUBLISHING   community experience distilled

BIRMINGHAM - MUMBAI

JavaFX Essentials

First published: June 2015

Production reference: 1250615

Published by Packt Publishing Ltd.
Livery Place
35 Livery Street
Birmingham B3 2PB, UK.

ISBN 978-1-78439-802-6

www.packtpub.com

Credits

Author
Mohamed Taman

Reviewers
Sergey Grinev

José Pereda

Commissioning Editor
Amarabha Banerjee

Acquisition Editor
Aaron Lazar

Content Development Editor
Sumeet Sawant

Technical Editor
Naveenkumar Jain

Copy Editors
Roshni Banerjee

Aditya Nair

Adithi Shetty

Project Coordinator
Shweta Birwatkar

Proofreader
Safis Editing

Indexer
Hemangini Bari

Graphics
Sheetal Aute

Production Coordinator
Nitesh Thakur

Cover Work
Nitesh Thakur

About the Author

Mohamed Taman, chief of architects and software development manager at e-finance, lives in Cairo, Egypt. He graduated in electrical engineering from Faculty of Engineering, Cairo University. He is an experienced Java developer who has worked on the Web, mobile, and IoT for industries, including finance, banking, tourism, government, and healthcare. Before that, he worked with Pfizer, Intercom Enterprise (a Gold IBM partner), Silicon Expert, and Oracle using varied technologies, such as user-facing GUI frontends, backends, mid-tiers, and integrations of large-scale systems.

He enjoys speaking at many conferences evangelizing Java standards and his experience worldwide, as he is a strong Java community member and a Java Champion since 2015.

In addition, Mohamed is a member of Adopts Java EE 8, OpenJDK, and JavaFX programs. He was an executive member of Java Community Process Organisation, being the first African to join its board.

He is also a member of the expert group JSR 354, 363, and 373. He is also the leader of EJUG and MoroccoJUG member, a board member of Oracle Egypt Architects Club. He won the 2014 Duke's choice and 11th annual JCP adopt 2013 awards.

You can read more about the author at `http://about.me/mohamedtaman`.

About the Reviewers

Sergey Grinev is an experienced software development and QA engineer focused on building reliable quality processes for Java platforms. He started to work in this area during his employment with Oracle, where he was responsible for JavaFX quality. Since the past few years, he has been working for Azul Systems on the quality of their custom JVMs.

Also, Sergey enjoys teaching people, presenting on various Java conferences, giving lessons, and answering Java-related questions on `http://stackoverflow.com`.

He graduated from St. Petersburg State University and currently resides in St. Petersburg, Russia.

José Pereda has done his PhD in structural engineering and works as an assistant professor in the School of Industrial Engineering at the University of Valladolid in Spain. His passion lies in applying programming to solve real problems. Working with Java since 1999, he is now a JavaFX advocate, developing commercial applications and open source projects (JFXtras, FXyz, `https://github.com/jperedadnr`), coauthoring a JavaFX book (*JavaFX 8 Introduction by Example*), blogging (`http://jperedadnr.blogspot.com.es/`), tweeting (`@JPeredaDnr`), and speaking at conferences (JavaOne, JAX, Jfokus, JavaLand, and so on). José lives with his wife and kids in Valladolid, Spain.

www.PacktPub.com

Support files, eBooks, discount offers, and more

For support files and downloads related to your book, please visit www.PacktPub.com.

Did you know that Packt offers eBook versions of every book published, with PDF and ePub files available? You can upgrade to the eBook version at www.PacktPub.com and as a print book customer, you are entitled to a discount on the eBook copy. Get in touch with us at service@packtpub.com for more details.

At www.PacktPub.com, you can also read a collection of free technical articles, sign up for a range of free newsletters, and receive exclusive discounts and offers on Packt books and eBooks.

https://www2.packtpub.com/books/subscription/packtlib

Do you need instant solutions to your IT questions? PacktLib is Packt's online digital book library. Here, you can search, access, and read Packt's entire library of books.

Why subscribe?

- Fully searchable across every book published by Packt
- Copy-and-paste, print, and bookmark content
- On-demand and accessible via a web browser

Free access for Packt account holders

If you have an account with Packt at www.PacktPub.com, you can use this to access PacktLib today and view nine entirely free books. Simply use your login credentials for immediate access.

Table of Contents

Preface

This book, as its title (*JavaFX 8 Essentials*) suggests, is a pragmatic book that provides you with a robust set of essential skills that will guide you to become confident enough to rapidly build high-performance JavaFX 8 client applications. These applications take advantage of modern GPUs through hardware-accelerated graphics while delivering a compelling, complex, and fancy rich-client GUI for your customer, which will impress them quite a bit.

Learning the JavaFX 8 essentials is the first step to plunging into creating applications that most importantly run on any platform, from the *desktop, Web, mobile, tablets*, to *embedded* devices such as *Arduino, Raspberry Pi*, and multi-core development. Following Java's *Write once, run anywhere* paradigm, JavaFX also preserves the same. Because JavaFX 8 is written totally from scratch in the Java language, you will feel at home.

Most of the chapters are a fast-paced guide that will help you get a head start on Java GUI programming, leveraging JavaFX 8 and deploying and running on any platform.

While working through the book examples, you will find code is written with JavaFX 8 on Java 8 (yes, Java SE 8) so that the new APIs and language enhancements will help you become a more productive developer. Having said this, it will be handy (and I encourage you to go for this) to explore all of the new Java 8 capabilities.

Finally, yet importantly, you will be able to develop amazing touch-less interactive motion applications with JavaFX that interact with Leap motion devices.

What this book covers

Chapter 1, Getting Started with JavaFX 8, is an introduction to JavaFX 8. It discusses JavaFX 8 as a technology, why you should care about it, its history, core features, and where it can be used.

So it is time to get ready with the right tools and go through the necessary steps to install JavaFX 8 and its supporting development tools. Learn about additional tools that will increase reader productivity in this chapter. As a final verification that we are on the right track, we are going to close the chapter with a simple Hello JavaFX application.

Chapter 2, JavaFX 8 Essentials and Creating a Custom UI, discusses how there is nothing more frustrating than receiving complicated advice as a solution to a problem. Because of this, I have always made it a point to focus on the essentials. In order to render graphics on the JavaFX scene, you will need a basic application, scene, canvas, shapes, text, controls, and colors.

Also, you will learn about JavaFX 8 essential application structures that serve as a backbone to any future application. And finally, we will also explore some Java SE 8 features (such as Lambda, Streams, JavaFX Properties, and so on) to help increase code readability, quality, and productivity.

After getting hands-on experience in creating a structured JavaFX 8 application, wouldn't it be nice if you could change the UI of your application without altering its functionality? In this chapter, you will learn about theming and how to customize applications by applying various themes (look and feel) and the fundamentals of JavaFX CSS styling.

You will use Scene Builder to create and define UI screens graphically and save them as a JavaFX FXML-formatted file. Finally, you will learn about creating custom controls.

Chapter 3, Developing a JavaFX Desktop and Web Application, covers on how to develop a compelling desktop and Web application that takes advantage of multi-core hardware accelerated GPUs to deliver a high performance UI-based application with an amazing appearance.

As JavaFX is totally written from the ground up in Java, some Java SE 8 built-in core libraries will be used to power our application. Also, you will learn how to package your application as a standalone application to be launched and distributed.

In addition, we will cover the essential core web APIs in any web application levered by JavaFX 8, such as `javafx.scene.web.WebEngine` and `javafx.scene.web.WebView`.

We will also discuss the relationship between JavaFX and HTML5, which is important because they complement each other. JavaFX's rich client APIs, coupled with HTML5's rich web content, create a user experience resembling a RIA Web application with the characteristics of native desktop software.

Chapter 4, Developing a JavaFX Application for Android, as we see a rise in non-pc clients, mobile phones and tablets are gaining market share. JavaFX 8 can deliver a rich client application for Web and desktop. If you write a JavaFX application, make sure you want it to run on as many devices as possible. This chapter will give you essential hands-on experience and knowledge about SDKs that allow users to create native applications for Android mobile phones.

Chapter 5, Developing a JavaFX Application for iOS, is an extension to the previous chapter. If you write a JavaFX application for Android, be sure you want it to run on as many iOS devices as possible. This chapter will give you essential hands-on experience and knowledge about SDKs that allow them to create native applications for Apple iOS.

Chapter 6, Running JavaFX Applications on the Raspberry Pi, will provide you with all the necessary skills and knowledge to develop a JavaFX 8 application that runs on a credit card-sized computer, the Raspberry Pi board. As the Internet of things (IoT) has become a hot topic of late. Java was made for the Internet of things literally.

Chapter 7, Monitoring and Controlling Arduino with JavaFX, covers another kind of Internet of everything (IoT). Arduino is an open-source electronics prototyping platform, delivering low-cost prototyping platforms to support both the do-it-yourself concept and the maker movement.

This chapter will provide you with all the necessary skills and knowledge to quickly use JavaFX along with an Arduino board to develop desktop applications for monitoring data coming from the real world or controlling real devices.

Chapter 8, Interactive Leap Motion Apps with JavaFX, will make you learn about gesture recognition. You will discover an awesome gadget, the Leap Motion device, which will allow a touch-less approach to develop enhanced JavaFX applications.

Machine user input interfaces are becoming increasingly less mouse-centric, in favor of multi-touch and even touch-less input. Gestures are one of the ways humans can communicate with machines naturally these days.

Appendix, Become a JavaFX Guru, will make you find many useful links and references that will help you gain further knowledge about all things JavaFX.

At the end of this chapter, make sure to check out the many frameworks, libraries, and projects that use JavaFX in production today.

What you need for this book

The examples given in this book utilize the latest release of Java SE 8 at the time of writing, namely the Java SE 8 update 45 JDK edition. Starting with Java SE 8, it comes pre-bundled with the JavaFX 8 that we use throughout this entire book. Also, NetBeans IDE version 8.0.2 is used as an Integrated Development Environment, as well as the JavaFX designer tool Gluon Scene Builder version 8, as general software and tools.

As each chapter is unique in its nature and requires specific software and hardware for the JavaFX 8 examples to run normally, this book provides all the required software, tools, and hardware with detailed explanation on how to install and configure them, in order to run JavaFX 8 examples smoothly.

Who this book is for

If you are a Java developer, an experienced Java Swing, Flash/Flex, SWT, or a web developer looking to take your client-side applications to the next level, this book is for you. This book will put you on the right track to begin creating a fancy, customizable, and compelling user interface.

Also, you will learn how to create high-performance rich client-side applications rapidly that run on any platform, be it desktop, web, mobile, or embedded systems, such as Raspberry Pi, Arduino, and applications based on the touch-less Leap Motion.

This book is a fast-paced guide that will help you get a head start on Java GUI programming leveraging JavaFX 8, deployed and runs on any platform.

Conventions

In this book, you will find a number of styles of text that distinguish between different kinds of information. Here are some examples of these styles, and an explanation of their meaning.

Code words in text, database table names, folder names, filenames, file extensions, pathnames, dummy URLs, user input, and Twitter handles are shown as follows: "We can include other contexts through the use of the include directive."

A block of code is set as follows:

```
btn.setOnAction(new EventHandler<ActionEvent>() {
  @Override
  public void handle(ActionEvent event) {
    message.setText("Hello World! JavaFX style :)");
  }
});
```

Any command-line input or output is written as follows:

$ gradle build

New terms and **important words** are shown in bold. Words that you see on the screen, in menus or dialog boxes for example, appear in the text like this: "Click on **Install** to begin the installation".

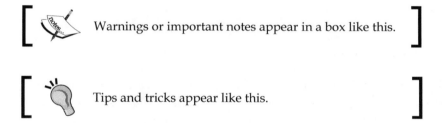

> Warnings or important notes appear in a box like this.

> Tips and tricks appear like this.

Reader feedback

Feedback from our readers is always welcome. Let us know what you think about this book — what you liked or may have disliked. Reader feedback is important for us to develop titles that you really get the most out of.

To send us general feedback, simply send an e-mail to feedback@packtpub.com, and mention the book title via the subject of your message.

If there is a topic that you have expertise in and you are interested in either writing or contributing to a book, see our author guide on www.packtpub.com/authors.

Customer support

Now that you are the proud owner of a Packt book, we have a number of things to help you to get the most from your purchase.

Downloading the example code

You can download the example code files for all Packt books you have purchased from your account at http://www.packtpub.com. If you purchased this book elsewhere, you can visit http://www.packtpub.com/support and register to have the files e-mailed directly to you.

Downloading the color images of this book

We also provide you with a PDF file that has color images of the screenshots/diagrams used in this book. The color images will help you better understand the changes in the output. You can download this file from http://www.packtpub.com/sites/default/files/downloads/8026OS_ColorImages.pdf.

Errata

Although we have taken every care to ensure the accuracy of our content, mistakes do happen. If you find a mistake in one of our books—maybe a mistake in the text or the code—we would be grateful if you would report this to us. By doing so, you can save other readers from frustration and help us improve subsequent versions of this book. If you find any errata, please report them by visiting http://www.packtpub.com/submit-errata, selecting your book, clicking on the **errata submission form** link, and entering the details of your errata. Once your errata are verified, your submission will be accepted and the errata will be uploaded on our website, or added to any list of existing errata, under the Errata section of that title. Any existing errata can be viewed by selecting your title from http://www.packtpub.com/support.

Piracy

Piracy of copyright material on the Internet is an ongoing problem across all media. At Packt, we take the protection of our copyright and licenses very seriously. If you come across any illegal copies of our works, in any form, on the Internet, please provide us with the location address or website name immediately so that we can pursue a remedy.

Please contact us at copyright@packtpub.com with a link to the suspected pirated material.

We appreciate your help in protecting our authors, and our ability to bring you valuable content.

Questions

You can contact us at questions@packtpub.com if you are having a problem with any aspect of the book, and we will do our best to address it.

Getting Started with JavaFX 8

1

JavaFX is Java's next-generation **Graphical User Interface (GUI)** toolkit. It's a platform that makes it easy to rapidly build high-performance Java client-side applications.

JavaFX's underlying engines take advantage of modern GPUs through hardware-accelerated graphics, while providing well-designed programming interfaces, thus enabling developers to combine graphics, animation, and UI controls.

These capabilities allow you to deliver a compelling, complex, and fully customizable client GUI for your customer that will make them quite impressed.

While the original targets of Java were the *embedded* and *client* worlds, since 2006, many reasons pushed the Java language to become the top development platform for the Enterprise world.

But recently, with the JavaFX platform's entrance as the standard client GUI, those original targets have started to gain popularity again.

Although it is much more than just a GUI toolkit, JavaFX allows Java developers to create client applications with compelling user interfaces that easily connect to backend systems.

In addition, JavaFX's flexible FXML support allows you to build **MVC (Model-View-Controller)** architectural pattern applications easily, and use the WYSIWYG approach using the Scene Builder tool.

JavaFX's bindings feature simplified communication between entities and support MVC even further. In addition to that, JavaFX provides fast, customizable UI modeling using CSS.

By adding a full-fledged `WebView` component with a document model, mapping to Java code is easy and provides great support for 3D and media capabilities.

In this chapter, we are going to cover the following topics:

- What is JavaFX and what are its targeted platforms?
- A walk through JavaFX history
- JavaFX goals, features, and what's new in JavaFX 8
- How to install Java SE 8, JavaFX 8, NetBeans, and configuring environment variables
- Developing a "*Hello World*" JavaFX 8 application, and understanding the JavaFX 8 basic application architecture and building blocks

JavaFX goals

JavaFX came to light with a primary goal – to be used across many types of devices, such as embedded devices, smartphones, TVs, tablet computers, and desktops. JavaFX also follows Java's *write once, run anywhere* paradigm.

JavaFX 8 is written totally from scratch in Java language, it makes you feel at home. Therefore, applications written in JavaFX can be deployed on desktops, laptops, the Web, embedded systems, mobiles, and tablets.

Embedded systems are no longer supported by Oracle; it is left to companies like ARM and others to support it. Mobile devices have never been supported from JavaFX 2.x to 8.x; the support exists now only because of **OpenJFX**. The community has benefitted from open source bringing JavaFX to mobile environments.

For more about OpenJFX, visit `https://wiki.openjdk.java.net/display/OpenJFX/Main`.

JavaFX is a set of graphics and a media package that enables developers to design, create, test, debug, and deploy rich client applications that operate consistently across diverse platforms, in one bundle, without the need for many separate libraries, frameworks, and APIs to achieve the same goal. These separate libraries include media, UI controls, `WebView`, 3D, and 2D APIs.

So if you are a Java frontend developer, an experienced Java Swing, Flash/Flex, SWT, or web developer looking to take your client-side applications to the next level, and you want to develop an attractive and complex user interface for your customer, then you are on track learning JavaFX skills – this book is for you.

Getting started

This chapter is an introduction to JavaFX 8; we have already talked about JavaFX 8 as a technology and why you should care about it.

Next, we will navigate its history, exploring its core features and where it could be used.

Before you start using this book to learn JavaFX 8, we will go through the preparation of your development environment by installing various required software bundles, to be able to compile and run many of its examples.

In this chapter, you will learn how to install the required software, such as the **Java Development Kit JDK** and the NetBeans **Integrated Development Environment (IDE)**.

After installing the required software, you will begin by creating a traditional *Hello JavaFX 8* example. Once you feel comfortable with the development environment, as a final verification that we are on the right track, we will walk through the Hello JavaFX 8 source code to understand the basic JavaFX 8 application architecture.

 If you are already familiar with the installation of the JDK and the NetBeans IDE, you can skip to *Chapter 2, JavaFX 8 Essentials and Creating a custom UI*, which covers JavaFX 8 fundamentals and how to create a custom UI component.

So what you are waiting for? Let's get started!

JavaFX history

You might believe JavaFX is quite a new technology, but it actually isn't. JavaFX has been here for a long time; unofficially since 2005. Ever since Sun Microsystems acquired the company *SeeBeyond*, there has been a graphics-rich scripting language known as **F3** (Form Follows Function), which was created by engineer Chris Oliver.

At the JavaOne 2007 conference, Sun Microsystems officially unveiled JavaFX as the language's name instead of F3. During the period 2007 to 2010, Oracle acquired many big companies like BEA Systems, JD Edwards, Siebel Systems, and so on. I was working for Oracle with the responsibility of integrating different customer support channels to the Oracle support website *MetaLink*, as it was called at that time.

On April 20, 2009, Oracle Corporation announced the acquisition of Sun Microsystems, making Oracle the new steward of JavaFX.

At JavaOne 2010, Oracle announced the JavaFX roadmap, which included its plans to phase out the JavaFX 1.3 scripting language and recreate the JavaFX platform for the Java platform as Java-based APIs. As promised, JavaFX 2.0 SDK was released at JavaOne in October 2011.

In addition to the release of JavaFX 2.0, Oracle took the platform to the next level by announcing its commitment to take steps to make JavaFX open source, thus allowing Java's versatile and strong community to help move the platform forward. Making JavaFX open source increased its adoption, enabled a quicker turnaround time on bug fixes, and generated new enhancements.

Between the versions JavaFX 2.1 and 2.2, the number of new features grew rapidly. JavaFX 2.1 was the official release of the Java SDK on Mac OS. JavaFX 2.2 was the official release of the Java SDK on the Linux operating system.

There was no such thing as JavaFX 3.x, but the big change in the Java development world happened with the Java SE 8 release, which was announced on March 18, 2014. Java SE 8 has many new APIs and language enhancements, which include **Lambdas**, Stream API, Nashorn JavaScript engine, and *JavaFX APIs*, which are being incorporated into standard JDK bundles, and JavaFX version becomes 8 as direct successor to JavaFX 2.0.

To see all of the new features in Java SE 8, visit `http://www.oracle.com/technetwork/java/javase/8-whats-new-2157071.html`.

When is JavaFX 8 available?

The answer is *now*. As mentioned before, Java SE 8 was released on March 18, 2014. For developers who use Java to build client-site applications, the JavaFX rich Internet application framework supports Java 8 now.

Most of the Java enterprise edition vendors support Java 8 too. Whether you move to Java SE 8 right away depends on the kind of projects you're working on.

In fact, as outlined in the Oracle JDK Support Roadmap, after April 2015, Oracle will not post further updates of Java SE 7 to its public download sites.

The JavaFX APIs are available as a fully integrated feature of the **Java SE Runtime Environment (JRE)** and JDK. The JDK is available for all major desktop platforms (*Windows*, *Mac OS X*, *Solaris*, and *Linux*), therefore JavaFX will also run on all major desktop platforms.

Relating to JavaFX 8, it supports the following APIs:

- 3D graphics
- Rich text support
- Printing APIs.

JavaFX features

The following features are included in JavaFX 8 and later releases as per JavaFX's official documentation:

- **Java APIs**: JavaFX is a Java library that consists of classes and interfaces that are written in Java code.

- **FXML and Scene Builder**: This is an XML-based declarative markup language for constructing a JavaFX application user interface. You can code in FXML or use JavaFX Scene Builder to interactively design the GUI. Scene Builder generates FXML markup that can be ported to an IDE like NetBeans, where you can add the business logic. Moreover, the FXML file that is generated can be used directly inside the JavaFX application.

- **WebView**: This is a web component that uses WebKit, an HTML render engine technology, to make it possible to embed web pages within a JavaFX application. JavaScript running in WebView can call Java APIs and vice-versa.

- **Swing/SWT interoperability**: The existing Swing and SWT applications can benefit from JavaFX features such as rich graphics, media playback, and embedded web content.

- **Built-in UI controls and CSS**: JavaFX provides all the major UI controls, and some extra uncommon controls like charts, pagination, and accordion that are required to develop a full-featured application. Components can be skinned with standard web technologies such as CSS.

- **3D graphics features**: Support for the 3D graphics library is included.

- **Canvas API**: You can draw directly inside a JavaFX scene area using the Canvas API, which consists of one graphical element (node).

- **Multitouch support**: Multitouch operations are supported based on the capabilities of the underlying platform.

- **Hardware-accelerated graphics pipeline**: JavaFX graphics are based on the graphics-rendering pipeline, *Prism*. The Prism engine smoothly and quickly renders JavaFX graphics when used with a supported graphics card or **graphics processing unit (GPU)**. If a system does not feature one of them, then Prism defaults to the software-rendering stack.

- **High-performance media engine**: This engine provides a stable, low-latency media framework that is based on the GStreamer multimedia framework. The playback of web multimedia content is supported with the media pipeline.

- **Self-contained deployment model**: Self-contained application packages have all of the application resources and a private copy of the Java and JavaFX runtimes. They are distributed as native installable packages and provide the same installation and launch experience as native applications for that operating system.

What's new in JavaFX 8

The following is a brief summary of the new features and significant product changes made in the JavaFX component of the Java SE 8 release:

- The new *Modena theme* is now the default theme for JavaFX applications.

- Support for additional HTML5 features, including Web Sockets, Web Workers, Web Fonts, and printing capabilities have been added.

- The API enables you to embed **Swing** content into JavaFX applications with the new SwingNode class, which improves the Swing interoperability feature.

- DatePicker, Spinner, and TableView built-in UI controls are now available.

- It provides the public JavaFX printing APIs through the javafx.print package.

- Support for Hi-DPI displays has been made available.

- CSS-styleable classes became public APIs.

- A scheduled service class has been introduced.

- The 3D graphics library has been enhanced with several new API classes.

- Major updates have been added to the *Camera API* class in this release.

- Now JavaFX 8 supports rich text capabilities. These include bidirectional and complex text scripts such as Thai and Hindi in UI controls, and multiline, multistyle text in text nodes.

- Dialogs and accessibility APIs are supported.

In *Appendix, Become a JavaFX Guru*, I have provided a list of all the references (links, books, magazines, articles, blogs, and tools) and real JavaFX 8 production applications you will need to become a JavaFX guru.

The following figure shows the `Ensemble8.jar` application built using JavaFX 8, showing examples dealing with various JavaFX 8 components, topics and concepts. More interestingly, the source code is available to learn from and modify – consult the last chapter to see how to install this application.

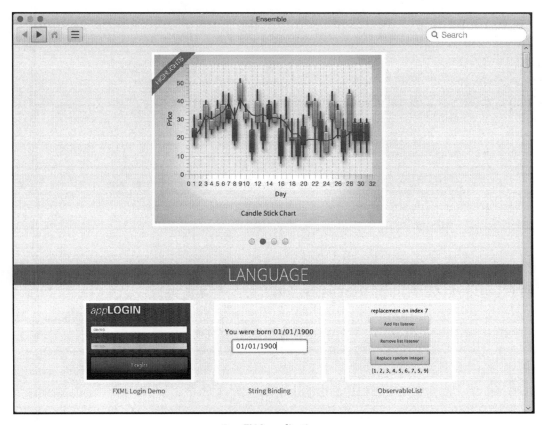

JavaFX 8 applications

There are many topics covered by the application, especially the new JavaFX 8 3D APIs, which can be found under the Graphics 3D section as seen in the following figure:

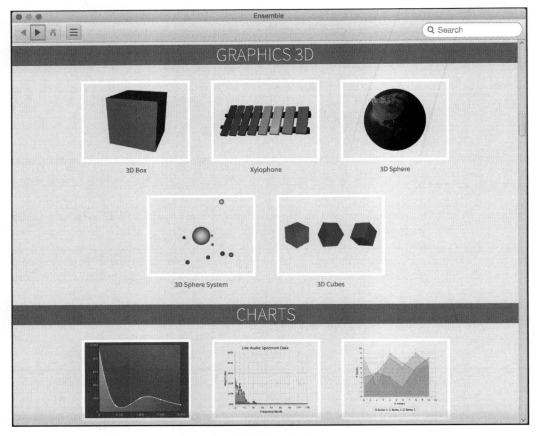

JavaFX 8 3D applications

Installing the required software

So far, we have had a good introduction to JavaFX and I am as eager as you to start creating and launching our first "Hello JavaFX 8" application. But this can't happen without downloading and installing the right tools that will allow us to create and compile most of the book's code.

You'll need to download and install *Java 8 Java Development Kit* (JDK) or a later version. Not the runtime version (JRE).

Download the latest Java SE 8u45 JDK or higher from the following location:

`http://www.oracle.com/technetwork/java/javase/downloads/index.html`

Download and install NetBeans 8.0.2 or higher from the following link `https://netbeans.org/downloads`, though the NetBeans IDE **All** Bundle is recommended, *you can use the Java EE bundle as well*, as shown in the figure:

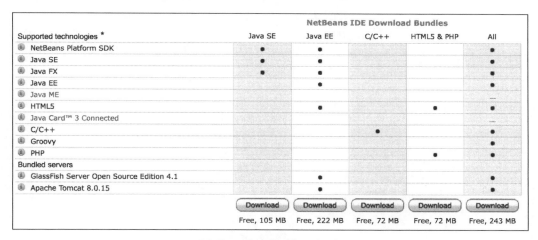

Supported technologies *	NetBeans IDE Download Bundles				
	Java SE	Java EE	C/C++	HTML5 & PHP	All
NetBeans Platform SDK	●	●			●
Java SE	●	●			●
Java FX	●	●			●
Java EE		●			●
Java ME					....
HTML5		●		●	●
Java Card™ 3 Connected					....
C/C++			●		●
Groovy					●
PHP				●	●
Bundled servers					
GlassFish Server Open Source Edition 4.1		●			●
Apache Tomcat 8.0.15		●			●
	Download	Download	Download	Download	Download
	Free, 105 MB	Free, 222 MB	Free, 72 MB	Free, 72 MB	Free, 243 MB

NetBeans bundles download.

Currently, JavaFX 8 runs on the following operating systems:

- Windows OS (XP, Vista, 7, 8) 32- and 64-bit
- Mac OS X (64-bit)
- Linux (32- and 64-bit), Linux ARMv6/7 VFP, HardFP ABI (32-bit)
- Solaris (32- and 64-bit)

Installing Java SE 8 JDK

The steps outlined in this section will guide you to successfully download and install Java SE 8. Download the Java SE 8 JDK from the following location:

`http://www.oracle.com/technetwork/java/javase/downloads/jdk8-downloads-2133151.html`

In the following steps, the Java SE 8u45 JDK 64-bit version (at the time of writing) on the Mac OS X Yosemite (10.10.3) operating system will be used as an example.

The steps are similar on other operating systems and JDK versions. However, if your environment is different, refer to the following link for additional details:

`http://docs.oracle.com/javase/8/docs/technotes/guides/install/toc.html`

The following are steps to install the Java SE 8 JDK:

1. Install the Java 8 JDK by launching the image file `jdk-8u45-macosx-x64.dmg`. A screen will appear that looks like the following screenshot once you've launched the JDK 8 setup image file. That's the package setup file. Double-click on it and the installer will launch:

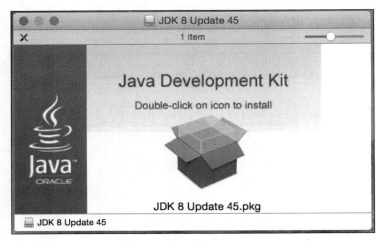

JDK 8 setup image file

 Typically, you will need administrator rights on the machine to install the software.

2. Begin the setup of the Java 8 JDK. The screen in the following screenshot will appear at the beginning of the installation process. Click on the **Continue** button, next on the **Installation** type screen wizard, click on **Install** to begin the installation.

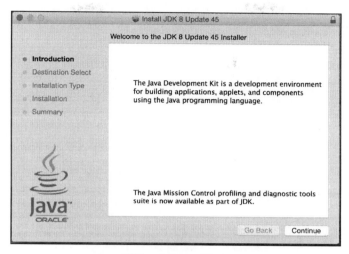

Java SE Development Kit 8 setup

3. Once you hit **Install**, you may be asked to supply your password. Supply it, click on **Ok** and the installation will proceed with a progress bar, as shown in following figure:

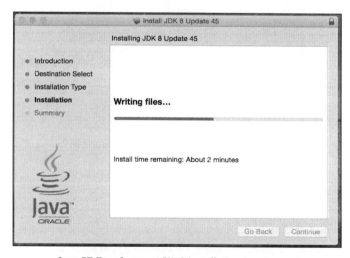

Java SE Development Kit 8 installation in progress

4. The setup will complete the installation of the Java 8 SE Development Kit. click on the **Close** button to exit.

Setting environment variables

Now you need to set a couple of key environment variables. How you set them and the values they should be set to vary depending on your operating system. The two variables to be set are:

- **JAVA_HOME**: This tells your operating system where the Java installation directory is.
- **PATH**: This specifies where the Java executable directory resides. This environment variable lets the system search paths or directories containing executable files. The Java executables reside in the bin directory under the JAVA_HOME home directory.

To make JAVA_HOME and PATH more permanent, you will want to add them to your system in such a way that they are always made available whenever you boot or log in. Depending on your operating system, you will need to be able to edit environment variable names and values.

In the *Windows environment*, you can use the keyboard shortcut *Windows logo key + Pause/Break key* and then click on **Advanced system settings** to display the **Systems Property** dialog.

Next, click on **Environment Variables**. This is where you can add, edit, and delete environment variables. You will add or edit the JAVA_HOME environment variable by using the installed home directory as the value. Shown in this screenshot is the Environment Variables dialog on the Windows operating system:

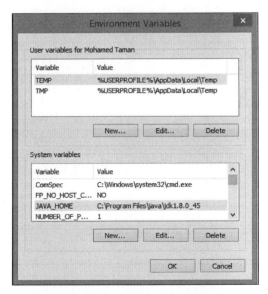

Windows Environment Variables

Let's set the environment variables:

- To set your JAVA_HOME environment variable for the **Mac OS X** platform, you will need to launch a terminal window to edit your home directory's .bash_profile file by adding the following export command:

  ```
  export JAVA_HOME=$(/usr/libexec/java_home -v 1.8)
  ```

- On **Linux** and other **Unix** operating systems that use Bash shell environments, launch a terminal window and edit either the ~/.bashrc or ~/.profile file to contain the export commands:

  ```
  export JAVA_HOME=/usr/java/jdk1.8.0
  export PATH=$PATH:$JAVA_HOME/bin
  ```

- On Linux and other Unix operating systems that use C shell (csh) environments, launch a terminal window and edit either the ~/.cshrc or ~/.login file to contain the setenv commands:

  ```
  setenv JAVA_HOME /usr/java/jdk1.8.0_45
  setenv PATH ${JAVA_HOME}/bin:${PATH}
  ```

Once you've set up your path and the JAVA_HOME environment variables, you will want to verify your setup by launching a terminal window and executing the following two commands from the command prompt:

```
java -version
javac -version
```

 The output in each case should display a message indicating the Java SE 8 version of the language and runtime.

Installing the NetBeans IDE

When developing JavaFX applications, you will be using the NetBeans IDE (or any other IDE of your preference). Be sure to download the correct NetBeans version containing JavaFX. To install the NetBeans IDE, follow these steps:

1. Download the NetBeans IDE 8.0.2 or later from the following location:

   https://netbeans.org/downloads/index.html

2. Launch the .dmg image file netbeans-8.0.2-macosx.dmg. The image will be verified and a folder containing the installer package archive, netbeans-8.0.2.pkg, will open; double-click on it to launch the installer. A dialog box will appear with the message: *This package will run a program to determine if the software can be installed.* Click on the **Continue** button.

3. Once you've launched the NetBeans installation dialog, click on **continue** again. Next, accept the license and click on **Continue** and then on **Agree**.

4. Click on the **Install** button to proceed. The following screenshot shows a **Mac** security warning prompt; supply your password and click on **Install Software**.

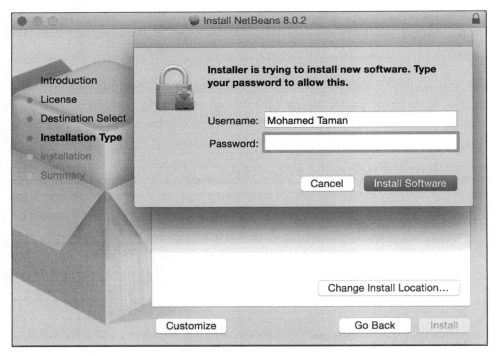

The Mac Security Warning dialog

5. The NetBeans IDE installation processes will begin. The following screenshot shows the installation progress bar:

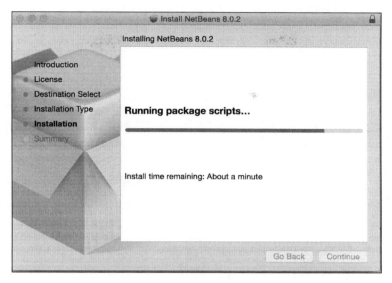

Installation progress

6. Click on the **Close** button to complete the installation, as shown here:

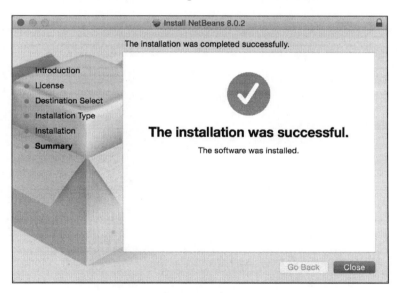

Setup complete

Now you are ready to move on and create JavaFX applications.

Creating "Hello World" JavaFX-style applications

The best way to show you what it is like to create and build a JavaFX application would be with a Hello World application.

In this section, you will be using the NetBeans IDE we just installed to develop, compile, and run a JavaFX-based Hello World application.

Using the Netbeans IDE

To quickly get started with creating, coding, compiling, and running a simple JavaFX-style Hello World application using the NetBeans IDE, follow the steps outlined in this section:

1. From the **File** menu, choose **New Project**.

2. From **JavaFX application category**, choose **JavaFX Application**. Click on **Next**.

3. Name the project HelloJavaFX. Optionally, you can define the package structure for application classes. Then click on **Finish** as shown in the following screenshot:

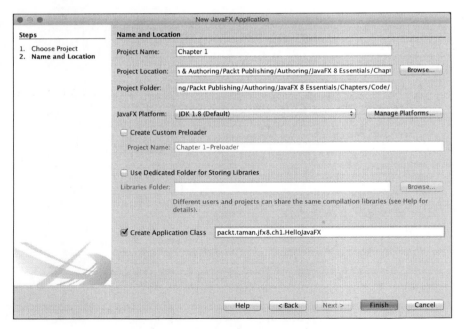

New JavaFX application wizard

NetBeans opens the `HelloJavaFX.java` file and populates it with the code for a basic "Hello World" application.

You will find that this version of code has been modified a bit from the one NetBeans actually creates, and you can compare them to find differences, but they have the same structure. I did that to show the result on the text node on the `Scene` instead of the console when clicking on the **Say 'Hello World'** button. For that, a `VBox` container has also been used.

4. Right-click on the project and click on **Run** from the menu as shown here:

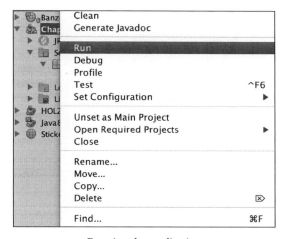

Running the application

5. NetBeans will compile and run the application. The output should be as shown in the following screenshot:

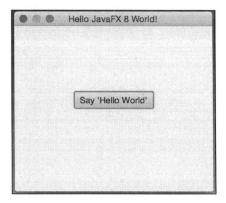

JavaFX Hello World launched from the NetBeans IDE

6. Click on the button and you should see the following result:

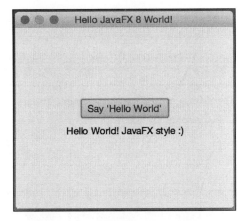

JavaFX Hello World results

Here is the modified code of the basic Hello world application (`HelloJavaFX.java`):

```java
import javafx.application.Application;
import javafx.scene.Scene;
import javafx.scene.control.Button;
import javafx.scene.text.Text;
import javafx.stage.Stage;
import static javafx.geometry.Pos.CENTER;
import javafx.scene.layout.VBox;

/**
  * @author mohamed_taman
  */
public class HelloJavaFX extends Application {

  @Override
  public void start(Stage primaryStage) {

    Button btn = new Button();
    Text message = new Text();

    btn.setText("Say 'Hello World'");

    btn.setOnAction(event -> {
      message.setText("Hello World! JavaFX style :)");
    });
```

```
        VBox root = new VBox(10,btn,message);
        root.setAlignment(CENTER);

        Scene scene = new Scene(root, 300, 250);

        primaryStage.setTitle("Hello JavaFX 8 World!");
        primaryStage.setScene(scene);
        primaryStage.show();
    }
    public static void main(String[] args) {
        launch(args);
    }
}
```

How it works

Here are the important things to know about the basic structure of a
JavaFX application:

- The main class for a JavaFX application should extend the `javafx.`
  `application.Application` class. The `start()` method is the *main*
  entry point for all JavaFX applications.

- A JavaFX application defines the user interface container by means of
  a *stage* and a *scene*. The JavaFX `Stage` class is the top-level JavaFX container.
  The JavaFX `Scene` class is the container for all content. The following code
  snippet creates a stage and scene and makes the scene visible in a given pixel
  size – `new Scene(root, 300, 250)`.

- In JavaFX, the content of the scene is represented as a hierarchical scene
  graph of nodes. In this example, the root node is a `VBox` layout object, which
  is a resizable layout node. This means that the root node's size tracks the
  scene's size and changes when a user resizes the stage.

- The `VBox` is used here as the container that arranges its content nodes
  vertically in a single column with multiple rows. We have added the button
  btn control to the first row in the column, then the text **message** control to
  the second row on the same column, with vertical space of 10 pixels, as in the
  following code snippet:

```
VBox root = new VBox(10,btn,message);
root.setAlignment(CENTER);
```

- We set the button control with text, plus an event handler to set the message text control to **Hello World! JavaFX style :)** when the button is clicked on.

- You might note a strange code syntax written in Java, with no compiler errors. This is a **Lambda** expression, which has been added to Java SE 8, and we are going to talk about it briefly in *Chapter 2, JavaFX 8 Essentials and Creating a custom UI*. With a slight comparison to old anonymous inner classes style, it is cleaner and more concise to use Lambda expression now. Have a look at this comparison of code:

Old School:

```
btn.setOnAction(new EventHandler<ActionEvent>() {
  @Override
  public void handle(ActionEvent event) {
    message.setText("Hello World! JavaFX style :)");
  }
});
```

New Era:

```
btn.setOnAction(event -> {
    message.setText("Hello World! JavaFX style :)");
});
```

- The main() method is not required for JavaFX applications when the **JAR** file for the application is created with the JavaFX Packager tool, which embeds the JavaFX Launcher in the JAR file.

- However, it is useful to include the main() method so you can run JAR files that were created without the JavaFX Launcher, such as when using an IDE in which the JavaFX tools are not fully integrated. Also, **Swing** applications that embed JavaFX code require the main() method.

- Here, in our main() method's entry point, we launch the JavaFX application by simply passing in the command-line arguments to the Application.launch() method.

- After the Application.launch() method has executed, the application will enter a ready state and the framework internals will invoke the start() method to begin.

- At this point, the program execution occurs on the *JavaFX application thread* and not on the **main thread**. When the start() method is invoked, a JavaFX javafx.stage.Stage object is available for you to use and manipulate.

Advanced topics will be discussed at length in the next chapters. More importantly, we will go through the JavaFX application thread in the coming chapters. In the last three chapters, we will see how to bring the result from other threads into the JavaFX application thread in order to render it correctly on the scene.

Summary

So far, you have learned what JavaFX is and seen its power. You have managed to download and install both Java 8 JDK and NetBeans IDE. After successfully installing the prerequisite software, you created a JavaFX Hello World GUI application through the NetBeans IDE. After learning how to compile and run a JavaFX application, you did a quick code walkthrough of the source file `HelloJavaFX.java`.

Next, in *Chapter 2, JavaFX 8 Essentials and Creating a custom* you'll learn about JavaFX 8 architecture components and engines, which allow JavaFX applications to run efficiently and smoothly under the hood. You will also learn about the most common layout UI components and get an idea about theming your application as a whole or as individual scene nodes.

We will also be covering Java SE 8's most important feature, Lambda expressions, and how it works. We will then get insights into **Scene Builder** as a declarative UI and productive tool, then learn about generated FXML-based markup document and how to import it into NetBeans IDE to continue your application logic implementation to associate it to the already declared UI controls inside your FXML document.

Finally, you will be able to create a custom UI component that isn't bundled with default JavaFX 8 UI controls.

2
JavaFX 8 Essentials and Creating a Custom UI

Getting to know the essentials of JavaFX will definitely help you to easily build complicated and complex UI solutions.

In this chapter, you will get a brief introduction about JavaFX 8 architecture, so you get an idea of how JavaFX architecture components and engines interconnect together with your JavaFX application efficiently and render its graphics smoothly.

You will learn how to render graphics on the JavaFX scene and, for that, we will create a basic application using a scene, some controls, and styling.

We will touch upon the fundamentals of Java SE 8 features (such as **Lambda** and **functional interfaces**) to help increase code readability, quality, and productivity.

Once we have our first structured JavaFX 8 application, wouldn't it be nice if you could change the UI of your application without altering its functionality? You will learn about theming by having a glance at the fundamentals of JavaFX CSS styling.

Finally, you will find out how to use Scene Builder to create and define UI screens graphically and save them as a JavaFX FXML-formatted file. And you will get hands-on experience of creating *custom controls*.

In this chapter, we'll cover the following topics:

- Understanding JavaFX architecture components
- Using JavaFX components to set up the UI
- Using Java SE 8, Lambda expressions, and other features

- Theming your application to target different platforms
- Customizing the application UI with CSS
- Using the Scene Builder tool to create the UI visually
- Building a custom UI with FXML

Quick review of the JavaFX 8 architecture

To better understand how the framework's components and engines interact together to run your JavaFX application, this section gives a high-level description of the JavaFX architecture and ecosystem.

The following figure illustrates the JavaFX platform's architectural components. It displays each component and how each of them interconnects.

The engine that is responsible for running your JavaFX application code lies below the JavaFX public APIs.

This engine is composed of subcomponents. These include **Prism**, a JavaFX high-performance graphics engine; the Glass toolkit, a small and efficient windowing system; a media engine; and a web engine.

 While these components are not exposed through public APIs, we will describe them so you have a better idea of what makes JavaFX applications run successfully in an efficient way.

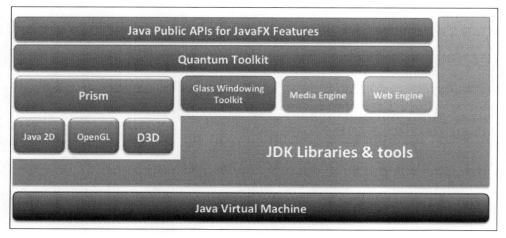

JavaFX architecture diagram

For more information and a description of the JavaFX architecture and ecosystem, visit http://docs.oracle.com/javase/8/javafx/get-started-tutorial/jfx-architecture.htm.

Scene graphs

Every application has a starting root point to construct a UI hierarchy, and the starting point for JavaFX applications is the *scene graph*. In the preceding screenshot, it is shown as part of the top layer in blue. It is the root tree of nodes that represents all of the visual elements of the application's user interface. It also tracks and handles any user input and can be rendered, as it is itself a UI node.

Node is any single element in the scene graph tree. Each node has these properties by default – an ID for identification, a list of style classes for changing its visual properties, and a bounding volume to fit correctly on the scene with other components and inside its parent layout container node, with the exception of the root node of a scene graph.

Each node in a scene graph tree has a single parent but could have zero or more children; however, the scene root has no parent (is null). Moreover, JavaFX has a mechanism to ensure a node could have only a single parent; it can also have the following:

- Visual effects, such as blurs and shadows
- Controlling components transparency via opacity
- CPU-accelerated 2D transforms, transitions, and rotations
- 3D transforms such as transitions, scaling, and rotations
- Event handlers (such as mouse events, key events, or other input methods such as touch events)
- An application-specific state

The following figure shows the relationship between the stage, scene, UI nodes, and graphical tree:

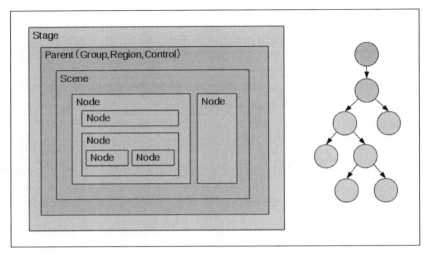

JavaFX UI tree hierarchy relationship

The graphics primitives also are an integral part of the JavaFX scene graph, such as lines, rectangles, and text in addition to images, media, UI controls, and layout containers.

When it comes to delivering complex and rich UIs for customers, scene graphs simplify this task. Also, you can use the `javafx.animation` APIs to quickly and easily animate various graphics in the scene graph.

In addition to these features, the `javafx.scene` API allows the creation and specification of several content types as the following:

- **Nodes**: Any node element represented as UI controls, charts, groups, containers, embedded web browser, shapes (2-D and 3-D), images, media, and text

- **Effects**: These are simple objects that, when applied to a UI node, change its appearance on the scene graph node, such as blurs, shadows, and color adjustment

- **State**: Any application-specific state such as transforms (positioning and orientation of nodes) and visual effects

Java public APIs for JavaFX features

This is your Swiss-knife toolkit provided as a complete set of Java public APIs that support rich client application development.

These APIs provide you with unprecedented flexibility to construct your rich client UI applications by combining the best capabilities of the Java SE platform with comprehensive, immersive media functionality into an intuitive and comprehensive one-stop development environment at hand.

These Java APIs for JavaFX allow you to do the following:

- Use the powerful features of Java SE, from generics, annotations, and multithreading, to new Lambda Expressions (introduced in Java SE 8).

- Provides an easier way for web developers to use JavaFX from other JVM-based dynamic languages, such as *JavaScript*.

- Writing large and complex JavaFX applications by integrating other system languages, such as *Groovy*.

- Binding your UI controls to your controller attributes for automatic notifications and updates to be reflected from your model to bound UI nodes. Binding includes support for high-performance lazy binding, binding expressions, bound sequence expressions, and partial bind reevaluation. We will see this in action and more in *Chapter 3, Developing a JavaFX Desktop and Web Application*.

- Introducing observable lists and maps, which allow applications to wire UIs to data models to observe the changes in those data models and update the corresponding UI control accordingly by extending the Java collections library.

Graphics System

The JavaFX Graphics System, shown in Purple in the preceding figure, supports both 2D and 3D scene graphs to run smoothly on the JavaFX scene graph layer. As it is the implementation detail beneath this layer, it provides the rendering software stack when running on a system that doesn't have sufficient graphics hardware to support hardware-accelerated rendering.

The JavaFX platform has two graphics-accelerated pipelines that implement:

- **Prism**: This is the engine that processes all render jobs. It can run on both hardware and software renderers, including 3D. Rasterization and rendering of JavaFX scenes are taken care of by this engine. Based on the device being used, the following multiple render paths are possible:
    - ○ DirectX 9 on Windows XP and Vista, and DirectX 11 on Windows 7
    - ○ OpenGL on Linux, Mac, and Embedded
    - ○ Software rendering when hardware acceleration is not possible
- **Quantum Toolkit**: This is responsible for linking the Prism engine and Glass Windowing Toolkit together to make them available to the JavaFX layer above them in the stack. This is in addition to managing any threading rules related to rendering versus event handling.

Glass Windowing Toolkit

The Glass Windowing Toolkit, shown in red in the middle portion of the preceding figure, serves as the platform-dependent layer that connects the JavaFX platform to the native operating system.

As its main responsibility is to provide native operating services, such as managing the timers, windows, and surfaces, its position in the rendering stack is the lowest.

JavaFX threads

Normally, the system runs two or more of the following threads at any given time:

- **JavaFX application thread**: This is the main and primary thread used by the JavaFX application to run.
- **Prism render thread**: This handles rendering separately from the event dispatcher. It renders frame N while frame N +1 is being prepared to process next. Its big advantage is the ability to perform concurrent processing, especially on modern systems that have multiple processors.
- **Media thread**: This runs in the background and synchronizes the latest frames through the scene graph by using the JavaFX application thread.
- **Pulse**: This enables you to have a way to handle events asynchronously. It helps you manage synchronization between the JavaFX scene graph elements state and an event of the scene graph with the Prism engine. When it is fired, the state of the elements on the scene graph is synchronized to the rendering layer.

Any Layout nodes and CSS are also tied to pulse events.

The *Glass Windowing Toolkit* executes all pulse events using high-resolution native timers to make the execution.

Media and images

The JavaFX `javafx.scene.media` APIs provide media functionality. JavaFX supports both visual and audio media. For audio files, it supports MP3, AIFF, and WAV files and FLV video files.

You can access your media functionalities through three main separate components provided by JavaFX media – the `Media` object represents a media file, `MediaPlayer` plays a media file, and `MediaView` is a node that displays the media into your scene graph.

 The Media Engine component, shown in orange in the preceding figure, has been designed carefully with stability and performance in mind to provide a consistent behavior across all supported platforms.

Web component

The web engine component, shown in green in the preceding figure, is one of the most important JavaFX UI controls and is built based on the WebKit engine, which is an open source web browser engine that supports HTML5, JavaScript, CSS, DOM rendering, and SVG graphics. It provides a web viewer and full browsing functionality through its API. We will dive deep into this in *Chapter 3, Developing a JavaFX Desktop and Web Application*, when developing web applications.

It allows you to add and implement the following features in your Java applications:

- Render any HTML content from a local or remote URL
- Provide Back and Forward navigation, and support history
- Reload the content for any updates
- Animate and apply CSS effects to the web component
- Provide rich editing control for HTML content
- Can execute JavaScript commands and handle web control events

Layout components

When building a rich and complex UI, we need a way to allow for flexible and dynamic arrangements of the UI controls within the JavaFX application. This is the best place to use Layout containers or panes.

The Layout API includes the following container classes that automate common layout UI patterns:

- **BorderPane**: This lays out its content nodes in the top, bottom, right, left, or center region

- **HBox**: This arranges its content nodes horizontally in a single row

- **VBox**: This arranges its content nodes vertically in a single column

- **StackPane**: This places its content nodes in a back-to-front single stack at the center of the pane

- **GridPane**: This enable the creation of a flexible grid of rows and columns in which to lay out content nodes

- **FlowPane**: This arranges its content nodes in either a horizontal or vertical flow, wrapping at the specified width (for horizontal) or height (for vertical) boundaries

- **TilePane**: This places its content nodes in uniformly sized layout cells or tiles

- **AnchorPane**: This enables the creation of anchor nodes to the top, bottom, left-hand side, or center of the layout, and we can freely position its child nodes

 Different containers can be nested within a JavaFX application; to achieve the desired layout structure, we will see this in action next when developing our Custom UI.

JavaFX controls

JavaFX controls are the building blocks of your UI layout, and they reside in the `javafx.scene.control` package as a set of JavaFX APIs. They are built by using nodes in the scene graph. They can be themed and skinned by JavaFX CSS. They are portable *across different platforms*. They take full advantage of the visually rich features of the JavaFX platform.

This figure shows some of the UI controls that are currently supported and there are more not shown here as well:

JavaFX UI controls sample

 For more detailed information about all the available JavaFX UI controls, see the official tutorial at `http://docs.oracle.com/javase/8/javafx/user-interface-tutorial/ui_controls.htm#JFXUI336` and the API documentation for the `javafx.scene.control` package.

Java SE 8 features

We will scratch the surface of Java SE 8 to understand two of the most important features – lambda or lambda expressions and functional interfaces, which make the lambdas available to us, to help write better, concise, and low-boilerplate JavaFX 8 code. However, keep in mind that we will not address every lambda detail in this book, as this is not a Java SE 8 book.

To get a better idea of Java's lambda roadmap, visit the following official tutorial: `http://docs.oracle.com/javase/ tutorial/java/javaOO/lambdaexpressions.html`.

Lambda expressions

The primary goal of project **lambda** in the Java language is to address the lack of functional programming and provide a way to do functional programming easily by creating anonymous (unnamed) functions in a similar manner to creating anonymous objects instead of methods in Java.

As you saw in the example from *Chapter 1, Getting Started with JavaFX 8*, we talked about the usual approach for defining a handler for the pressed event on a JavaFX button by using an anonymous inner class:

```
btn.setOnAction(new EventHandler<ActionEvent>() {
   @Override
   public void handle(ActionEvent event) {
     message.setText("Hello World! JavaFX style :)");
   }
});
```

This code is very verbose as compared to just wiring up a single line of code that sets the text attribute of the message text field in a button action. Wouldn't it be nice to be able to rewrite this block of code containing your logic without the need of so much boilerplate code?

Java SE 8 solves this with a Lambda expressions as follows:

```
btn.setOnAction(event -> {
    message.setText("Hello World! JavaFX style :)");
});
```

Beyond making your code more concise and easy to read, lambda expressions make your code perform better as well.

Syntax

There are two ways to write lambda expressions, and the general form is as shown in the following figure:

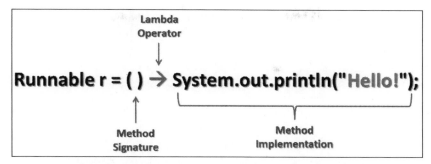

Lambda expression general form – creating a new thread as an example

These two ways are as follows:

- `(param1, param2, ...) -> expression;`
- `(param1, param2, ...) -> { /* code statements */ };`

The first form, the expression form, is used when we assign only one line of code or just a simple expression. While the second one, the block form, is a body of single or multiple lines of code, with a return statement, so we need to wrap them with curly braces.

The following three statements are equivalent:

- `btn.setOnAction((ActionEvent event) -> {message.setText("Hello World!");});`
- `btn.setOnAction( (event) -> message.setText("Hello World!"));`
- `btn.setOnAction(event -> message.setText("Hello World!"));`

To dive deeper into the new lambda expressions and their related features alongside the Java SE 8 features, I encourage you to try this articles series – Java SE 8 new features tour: `http://tamanmohamed.blogspot.com/2014/06/java-se-8-new-features-tour-big-change.html`

Functional interfaces

A lambda expression is fantastic, isn't it?, but you may be wondering what its exact type is, so it can be assigned to variables and passed to methods.

The answer is in the power of functional interfaces. How? Functional interfaces, cleverly created by Java language designers/architects as closures, use the concept of **Single Abstract Method (SAM)**, providing an interface with just one abstract method, and the @FunctionalInterface annotation. The single abstract method pattern is an integral part of Java SE 8's lambda expressions.

Let's clear things up with an example to illustrate the concept of both functional interfaces and lambda expressions. I have created a functional interface called Calculator.java containing a single abstract method, calculate(). Once it is created, you can declare and assign variables to lambda expressions. The following is the functional interface:

```
@FunctionalInterface
public interface Calculator {
    double calculate(double width, double height);
}
```

Now we are ready to create variables and assign them lambda expressions. The following code creates and assigns lambda expressions to our functional interface variables:

```
Calculator area = (width, height) -> width * height; //Area = w × h
//Perimeter = 2(w+h)
Calculator perimeter = (width, height) -> 2 * (height + width);
out.println("Rectangle area: "+ area.calculate(4, 5)+" cm.");
out.println("Rectangle perimeter: "+ perimeter.calculate(4, 5)+"
cm.");
```

The output of the code should be as follows:

```
Rectangle area: 20.0 cm.
Rectangle perimeter: 18.0 cm.
```

Theming

When working with designers and UX/UI specialists, you will hear about skinning the application or changing its appearance. Both terms are often interchangeable, and both of them reflect the basic concept of *theming*.

The idea of theming is to change the entire application style by changing its control appearance and without altering its underlying functionality.

In JavaFX, you have the ability to create, modify, or use existing themes to skin your applications, scene, or even just a UI control.

CSS

JavaFX **Cascading Style Sheets (CSS)** can be applied to any node in the JavaFX scene graph; they are applied to the nodes asynchronously. Styles can also be easily assigned to the scene at runtime, allowing an application's appearance to change dynamically.

It is based on the W3C CSS version 2.1 specifications, and is currently compatible with some additions from the current work on version 3. The JavaFX CSS support and extensions have been designed to allow JavaFX CSS style sheets to be parsed cleanly by any compliant CSS parser. This enables the mixing of CSS styles for JavaFX and for other purposes (such as for HTML pages) into a single style sheet.

All JavaFX property names are prefixed with an extension of -fx-, including those that might looks compatible with standard HTML CSS, because some JavaFX values have slightly different semantics from standard ones.

 For more about JavaFX CSS, see the Skinning JavaFX Applications with CSS document and the reference guide at http://docs.oracle.com/javase/8/javafx/api/ javafx/scene/doc-files/cssref.html.

Applying CSS theme

Here is a custom simple JavaFX CSS rule, ButtonStyle.css, that is to be used in our theming process to theme a button:

```
/* ButtonStyle.css */
.button {
-fx-text-fill: SKYBLUE;
-fx-border-color: rgba(255, 255, 255, .80);
-fx-border-radius: 8;
-fx-padding: 6 6 6 6;
-fx-font: bold italic 20pt "Arial";
}
```

We have two ways to apply CSS style sheets to change the look-and-feel theming of our JavaFX applications:

1. Using a JavaFX Application (`javafx.application.Application`) class static method `setUserAgentStylesheet(String URL)` method, which styles all the application hierarchy, including every scene and all child nodes in a JavaFX application. It is used as follows:

    ```
    Application.setUserAgentStylesheet(getClass().
    getResource("ButtonStyle.css").toExternalForm());
    ```

    Now you can use JavaFX 8's two style sheets that currently come preshipped, Caspian and Modena, and we can switch between them using the same method as shown here:

    ```
    // Switch to JavaFX 2.x's CASPIAN Look and Feel.
    Application.setUserAgentStylesheet(STYLESHEET_CASPIAN);

    // Switch to JavaFX 8's Modena Look and Feel.
    Application.setUserAgentStylesheet(STYLESHEET_MODENA);
    ```

     If you are invoking `setUserAgentStylesheet(null)` by passing a null value, the default look and feel will be loaded (in this case, Modena) whereas, if you are using JavaFX 2.x Caspian, the default one will be loaded.

2. Using scene's `getStylesheets().add(String URL)` method will style the individual scene and its child node automatically as follows:

    ```
    Application.setUserAgentStylesheet(null); // defaults to Modena
    // apply custom look and feel to the scene.
    scene.getStylesheets()
    .add(getClass().getResource("ButtonStyle.css")
    .toExternalForm());
    ```

    Basically, the default theme (Modena) will be loaded, as `Application.setUserAgentStylesheet(null)` is called. It then sets the scene's additional styling by invoking the `getStylesheets().add()` method.

Styles are first applied to the parent and then to its children. A node is styled after it is added to the scene graph, regardless of whether it's shown or not.

The JavaFX CSS implementation applies the following order of precedence – a style from a user agent style sheet has lower priority than a value set from code, which has lower priority than a Scene or Parent style sheet.

Inline styles have the highest precedence. Style sheets from a Parent instance are considered to be more specific than styles from Scene style sheets.

Scene Builder

For most complex and sophisticated UI requirements, wouldn't it be easier for designers to use a tool to design their UI with a WYSIWYG interface, without writing any code, and then load the result (FXML file) into their JavaFX application logic?

Therefore, you need JavaFX Scene Builder; it is a visual layout tool that allows you to easily lay out your UI controls so that you can quickly prototype your application with effects and animations. Scene Builder (version 2.0 upwards) is the compatible version for JavaFX 8.

At any time during the creation of your project, you can preview your work to check its real appearance before deploying it.

It is open source and therefore it integrates with most IDEs, but more tightly with the NetBeans IDE. It is also a cross-platform, self-contained application that runs on most platforms.

In addition to supporting CSS, it allows you to easily apply custom theming to your prototype.

Downloading and launching

At the beginning of 2015, Oracle release JavaFX Scene Builder tool version 2.0, and announced that it will no longer be providing builds of the JavaFX Scene Builder tool (in compiled form).

A company called **Gluon** (http://gluonhq.com) understands that tools can make or break a coding experience. So they have decided to begin providing builds, based on a fork they will maintain in a publicly accessible repository.

Gluon provides IDE plugins, as well as improved builds of the JavaFX Scene Builder tool based on the latest sources from OpenJFX, with additional improvements based on community involvement and a desire to better support third party projects such as **ControlsFX** (http://www.controlsfx.org/), **FXyz** (https://github.com/FXyz/FXyz), and **DataFX** (http://www.datafx.io/).

To get started let's download the tool from the following URL `http://gluonhq.com/products/downloads/`.

After downloading version 8.0 and installing it, launch it and the Scene Builder tool should open as in the following screenshot:

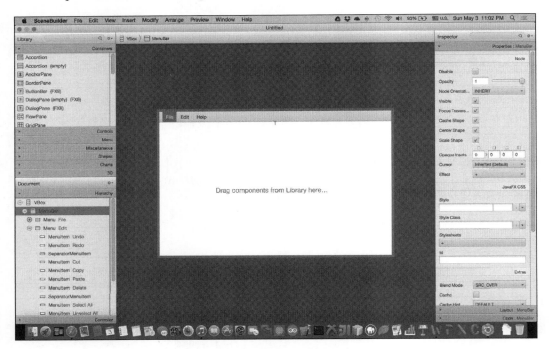

The JavaFX 8 Scene Builder tool.

FXML

While adding components and building your beautiful UI layout, Scene Builder under the hood generates a FXML - and XML-based markup file for you automatically, which will be used later to be bind your UI to your Java application logic.

One of the main advantages FXML provide is separation of concerns, as it decouples UI layer (*view*) from logic (*Controller*); this means you can alter UI at anytime without changing underlying logic. Since the FXML file is not compiled, it can be dynamically loaded at runtime without any required compilation. This means it helps you with rapid prototyping.

Loading FXML into JavaFX applications

It is very easy task to add your UI design after generating it from the Scene Builder tool. Shown here is code to load an FXML file in a `start()` method:

```
BorderPane root = new BorderPane();
Parent content = FXMLLoader.load(getClass().getResource("filename.
fxml"));
root.setCenter(content);
```

As you can see, I am using the static method load on the `javafx.fxml.`
`FXMLLoaderclass`, The `load()` method will load (`deserialize`) the FXML
file that was created by the Scene Builder tool.

Developing a custom UI

For the final part of this chapter, we are going to develop a custom UI component based on JavaFX 8 built-in controls.

We will develop this custom UI with concepts discussed before that are based on FXML; the primary advantage is the separation of concerns to customize the component later on without altering its functionality and any other logic bound to it.

The Login dialog custom UI

We will use most of the previously covered tools and techniques to develop our custom UI: the Login Dialog, which is a necessary component in every Enterprise application. Our UI component will be as shown in the following screenshot:

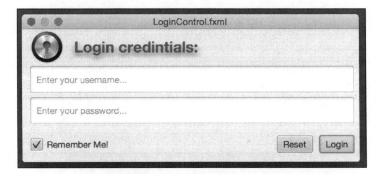

Login custom UI component

Structure of the Login dialog custom UI

The most common structure and stages in custom component development based on FXML markup are these:

- Develop the UI inside the Scene Builder tool; then export the result to the FXML-based file
- Extract the controller skeleton from the Scene builder
- Create a controller that binds the UI (view) to its logic and extends either a control or a layout
- Load the FXML file inside the Controller constructor
- Create an initialization method that makes sure that all FXML controls are initialized and loaded successfully
- Expose public attributes to get and set control data and action methods that need our implementation logic
- Develop a separate CSS file
- Use the custom component inside your application

Coding the Login dialog custom UI

Let's code and develop our custom UI, the Login Dialog:

1. Open the Scene Builder tool and create the UI. Its properties are as shown in the following figure:

2. The login dialog layout hierarchy will be as shown here:

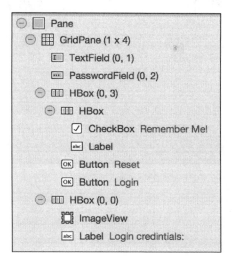

It consists of a Pane layout as the top and root layout node. Then, `GridPane(1,4)` is used to lay out the controls in a grid of one column and four rows using these:

- The **first** row contains the `HBox` layout control at location (`0,0`) to lay out the controls horizontally. It consists of the `ImageView` control to show the logo and Label for the title.

- The **second** row lays out the username `TextField` for the username attribute, at location (`0,1`).

- The **third** row lays out the password `PasswordField` for password attribute, at location (`0,2`).

- The **last** row, at location (`0,3`), has a root layout control `HBox`, and it lays out another HBox that contains the `CheckBox` and `Label` (for showing errors and other messages) controls aligned to the center-left. We then have two button controls, **Reset** and **Login**, which are aligned to the center-right.

     ○   In the Code tab, add a proper **fx:id** name to all of the controls in the dialog, and a name to onAction for buttons and checkbox events as in the following screenshot:

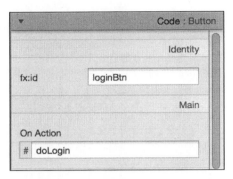

Login button properties

3. From the Scene Builder **Preview** menu, choose **Show preview in windows**. Your layout will pop up. If everything is okay and you are satisfied with the resulting design, from the menu bar, click on **File**, then **Save**, and enter the file name as LoginUI.fxml. Congratulations! You have created your first JavaFX UI layout.

4. Now we will open NetBeans to set up a JavaFX FXML project, so launch NetBeans, and from the **File** menu, choose **New Project**.

5. In the **JavaFX** category, choose **JavaFX FXML Application**. Click on **Next**. Then name the project **LoginControl**, change **FXML name** to LoginUI, and click on **Finish**.

 Make sure that the JavaFX platform is Java SE 8.

6. NetBeans will create a project structure as shown here:

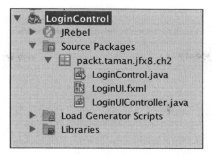

Login Control NetBeans project structure.

 Make sure to *clean and build* your project before running it, to avoid any problems you may face, especially when running your application and possibility loading the *.fxml file during runtime may return null.

7. Go to the Scene Builder tool and, from **View**, select **Show sample controller skeleton**. The window shown in the following screenshot will open, which we will copy to replace LoginUIController.java (this which extends the Pane class content code with the copied content in NetBeans) and then fix the missing imports.

8. Replace the previously generated and saved LoginUI.fxml file from Scene Builder with one already created by NetBeans.

9. Right-click on the LoginController.java file, choose **Refactor**, then **Rename**, and rename it to Main.java.

10. Finally, add the following code in the start(Stage stage) method of Main.java class as shown here. We are creating a new instance of the login component as a root node of our scene and adding it to the stage:

```
LoginUIController loginPane = new LoginUIController();

stage.setScene(new Scene(loginPane));
stage.setTitle("Login Dialog Control");
stage.setWidth(500);
```

```
stage.setHeight(220);
stage.show();
```

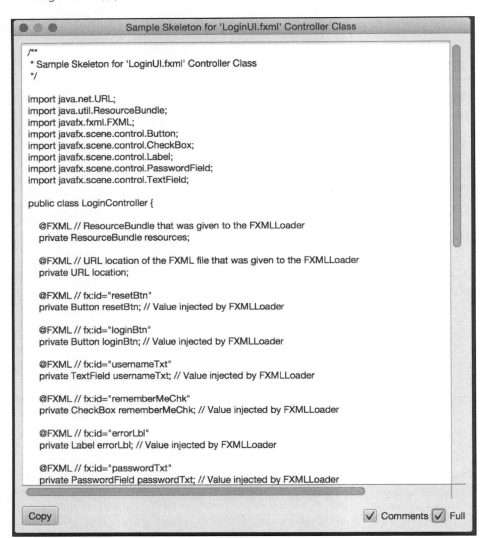

11. In the `LoginUIController.java` class, right-click under the class name and choose **Insert Code**; then choose **Constructor** and finally add the following code inside the constructor:

```
public LoginUIController() throws IOException {
  FXMLLoader fxmlLoader = new
    FXMLLoader(getClass().getResource("LoginUI.fxml"));
  fxmlLoader.setRoot(this);
  fxmlLoader.setController(this);
  fxmlLoader.load();
}
```

This code loads our `LoginUI.fxml` document and returns it as the Pane layout with its hierarchy. It then binds it to the current controller instance as the Controller and root node at the same time. Note that the controller extends Pane as the root element definition in `LoginUI.fxml`.

12. From NetBeans, choose **Clean and Build** and then right-click on the project and choose **Run**. The same screen we saw earlier should appear.

13. While the program is running, enter any credentials and click on the **Login** button; an error message will appear in red as shown in the following screenshot:

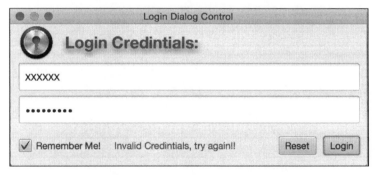

Login Control invalid login.

14. If the right credentials (user: *tamanm*, pass: *Tamanm*) are entered, the green message appears with "*Valid Credentials*", as shown in the following figure.

15. If the **Reset** button is clicked, then all controls return to the default values.

    Congratulations! You have successfully created and implemented a UI custom control.

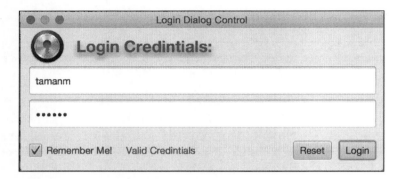

Summary

In this chapter, we have covered a lot of ground – getting started with a brief introduction about JavaFX 8 architecture components that act as the foundation layer to run your JavaFX application smoothly and efficiently. Then followed we explored how to render graphics on the scene with a brief explanation about the most common layouts and UI controls.

You were introduced to new features in Java SE 8 such as lambda expressions and functional interfaces, which was supported by examples showing the power of each.

You learned how to style your application with custom CSS files by using the `setUserAgentStylesheet(String URL)` and `getStylesheets().add(String URL)` methods. Next, you took a short look at the Scene Builder and how to load FXML into a scene. Finally, you learned about custom UI components in JavaFX and how to create them.

In the next chapter, you will learn how to create a desktop application that consists of multiple scenes and then how to package it. Additionally, we will learn how to interact with the Web and develop web applications using JavaFX 8.

3
Developing a JavaFX Desktop and Web Application

This chapter will cover how to develop compelling desktop and web applications that take advantage of the multicore, hardware-accelerated GPU to deliver high-performance UI-based applications that have an amazing look and feel.

As JavaFX is totally written from the ground up in Java, some Java SE 8 built-in core libraries will be used to power our application. In addition, we will learn how to package our application as a standalone application to be launched and distributed.

Also, we will cover the essential core web APIs in any web application levered by JavaFX 8, such as `javafx.scene.web.WebEngine`, `java.net.HttpURLConnection` and `javafx.scene.web.WebView`.

We will discuss the relationship between JavaFX and HTML5, which is important because JavaFX's APIs and the features of HTML5 complement one another. HTML5 is a platform for rich web content to create a user experience that resembles a **RIA (Rich Internet Application)** web application with the characteristics of native desktop software.

More importantly, we will go through the development of a desktop version of the *Note-taking Application* and then run it on the Web.

Additionally, we will cover all the required knowledge and skills to deploy the *Note-taking as a web application* on the desktop and the Web.

Here are the skills that will be learned during this chapter:

- Developing and running desktop and web applications
- Controlling application UIs
- How to package a JavaFX 8 desktop application
- Loading HTML5 content inside a JavaFX application
- Sending data from JavaFX to JavaScript and vice versa
- Deploying a JavaFX web application

Developing a note-taking application

Building an application for one platform just isn't good enough anymore. Desktop, Web, mobile, and embedded support are all required for a successful product, but learning the different environments is difficult. Here comes into play the power of JavaFX to write an application that will run on different platforms with simple tweaks, as we will see in this chapter.

Here, we are going to build a *note-taking* application for desktop and the Web as well. In this project, I'll show you how to create a complete JavaFX application from scratch using the JavaFX 8 SDK and the Java programming language using our previously installed developer tools (refer to *Chapter 1, Getting Started with JavaFX 8*).

I'll then show you how to create the application's two screen layouts and create the Java classes that control them. I'll create buttons that control navigation between different scenes, saves data, and then gets your UI controls updated dynamically with the power of property bindings.

The final project will look like the following screenshot:

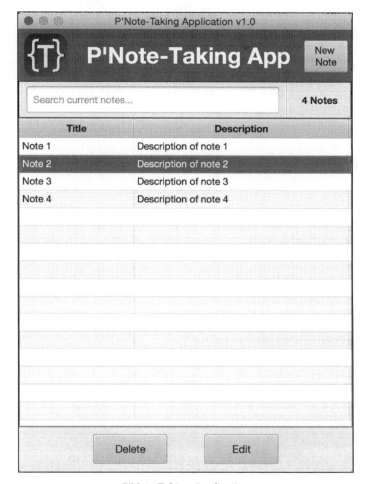

P'Note-Taking Application

This figure shows the add and edit screen opened from the main screen new note button to add new note, or edit button to edit one of listed notes as the following:

So, what are you waiting for? Let's go!

Building the UI prototype

The first step in building any successful application with **complex UI** (even simple ones) is prototyping your layout, screens relationship, their state, and their navigation. Sketch it on a piece of paper and then get feedback from your team and manager. Rework it and, once approved, start building a real interactive prototype for your customers, in order to get their feedback for final production.

This is what we are going to do now, and our application has been laid out on piece of paper on any easy to use UI sketcher tools as in the following image. We will then develop it with the Scene Builder tool as a complete prototype.

In addition, we are going to see the interoperability between NetBeans and the Scene builder tool.

 Note that it is easier to sketch your layout by drawing it on paper first, as it is a very quick way to edit, enhance, and figure out the final application layout before interacting with the tools to develop it.

Now, as we have sketched our application, we are ready to build our application's real prototype.

The best way to get the most out of the tools is to create your application skeleton (*controller classes and FXML base page definitions*) inside the NetBeans IDE, and then create and develop FXML pages inside the Scene builder tool. Here comes the powerful interoperability between the two tools.

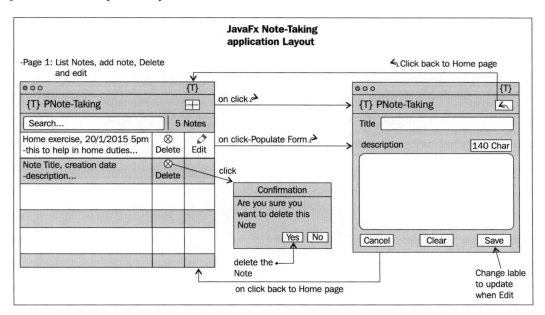

Here are the steps to start with JavaFX FXML application:

1. Open up the NetBeans IDE, and from the main menu, choose **File**, and then **New Project** a **New Project** dialog will open. From **Categories**, choose **JavaFX**, and then under **Projects**, choose JavaFX FXML Application. Then, click on the **Next** button:

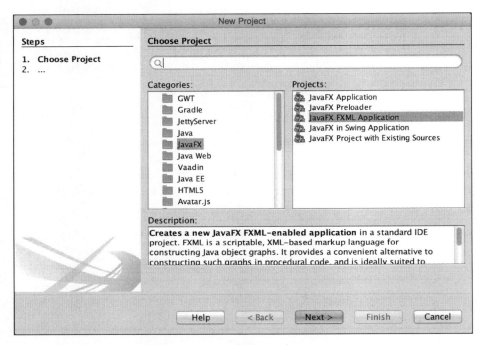

A new JavaFX FXML application

2. In the **JavaFX FXML application** dialog, add the relevant information. From **Project name**, add the location and **FXML name** (in my case, `ListNotesUI`). In **Create Application class**, I have added `packt.taman.jfx8.ch3.` `NoteTakingApp`, as shown in the following figure. Hit **Finish**.

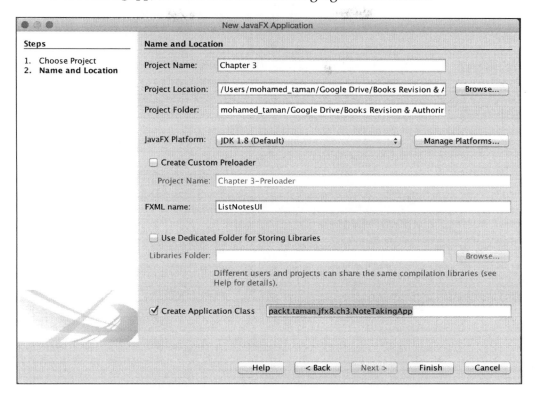

3. Now we have a project with the first FXML UI document (`ListNotesUI.fxml`), and we need to add the second FXML UI document (`AddEditUI.fxml`) alongside its controller.

4. To do that from the file, choose **New File**; then, under the **Categories** list, choose **JavaFX**, and from the **File Types** list, choose Empty FXML, and finally, click on **Next**, as shown in the following figure.

5. In the **New Empty FXML and Location** dialog, edit the **FXML Name** field to be AddEditUI, and then click on **Next**.

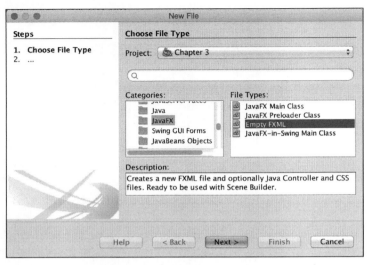

Adding a new empty FXML document

6. In the Controller Class dialog as in the following screen, tick the **Use Java Controller** checkbox. Make sure that **Create New Controller** has been selected, with the **Controller Name** as AddEditUIController. Then, click on **Next**, skip the **Cascading Style Sheet** dialog, and finally, click on **Finish**:

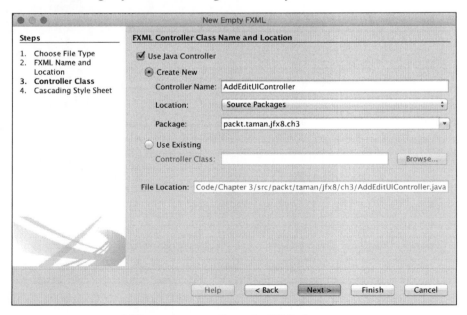

Adding a new controller to the FXML document

As we have built our project structure, it's time to add our controls into our pages UI using Scene Builder, similar to what we sketched on paper. To do so is easy:

1. From NetBeans, right-click on `ListNotesUI.fxml` and select Open or just double-click on it. **Scene Builder** will open with your FXML document in design mode.

 Note: It works only if Scene Builder is installed on your machine.

2. Design the page as per the following screenshot. Most importantly, don't forget to save your changes before returning back to NetBeans or closing **Scene Builder** for logic implementation.

Complete ListNotesUI.fxml document design

3. Perform the same steps for `AddEditUI.fxml`, and your design should end up like this:

Complete AddEditUI.fxml document design

You need to check the FXML document to see how we nested many containers and UI controls to achieve the desired UI we had sketched earlier, in addition to using their properties to control the spacing, alignment, font, and coloring.

Congratulations! You have converted your sketched layout to something vivid that could be presented as a project without logic to your team leaders and managers to get their feedback regarding colors, theming, and the final layout. Moreover, once it gets approved, you can proceed for the final customer feedback before diving deeper into the business logic.

Bringing your application to life – adding interactions

After designing your application, you need to bring it to life by making it more interactive and responsive to the functionality it is supposed to perform and act on the customer's proposed functional requirement.

The first thing I always do is to add the navigation handler from page to page, and I have done that in each FXML document controller class.

To eliminate redundancy and be modular, I have created a base navigation method in the `BaseController.java` class, which will be extended by all controllers in the system. This class will be useful for adding any common functionality and shared attributes.

The following method, `navigate(Event event, URL fxmlDocName)`, is one of the most important pieces of code that will be used in all of our system navigation (the comments illustrate the working mechanism):

```
protected void navigate(Event event, URL fxmlDocName) throws
   IOException {
   //Loading new fxml UI document
   Parent pageParent = FXMLLoader.load(fxmlDocName);
   //Creating new scene
   Scene scene = new Scene(pageParent);
   //get current stage
   Stage appStage = (Stage)((Node) event.getSource()).
     getScene().getWindow();
   //Hide old stage
   appStage.hide(); // Optional
   //Set stage with new Scene
   appStage.setScene(scene);
   //Show up the stage
   appStage.show();
}
```

This method will be called from the action handler of the **New Note** and edit button in the `ListNotesUI.fxml` page at `ListNotesUIController.java` and the **List Notes**, save, and **Cancel** buttons in the `AddEditUI.fxml` page at `AddEditUIController.java` as the following respectively.

Pay attention to the relationship between buttons defined in the FXML document and the controller. The @FXML annotation comes into play here to bind FXML attributes (*using #)* with the defined actions in the controller:

The **New Note** button definition in the `ListNotesUI.fxml` file is as follows:

```
<Button alignment="TOP_CENTER"
        contentDisplay="TEXT_ONLY"
        mnemonicParsing="false"
        onAction="#newNote"
```

```
        text="New Note"
        textAlignment="CENTER"
        wrapText="true"
/>
```

The **New Note** action is defined in `ListNotesUIController.java`, bound to the preceding button using `onAction="#newNote"`:

```
@FXML
 private void newNote(ActionEvent event) throws IOException {
        editNote = null;
        navigate(event, ADD.getPage());
 }
```

The **Back** button definition in the `AddEditUI.fxml` file is as follows:

```
<Button alignment="TOP_CENTER"
        contentDisplay="TEXT_ONLY"
        mnemonicParsing="false"
        onAction="#back"
        text="Notes List"
        textAlignment="CENTER"
        wrapText="true"
/>
```

The **Back** action is defined in `AddEditUIController.java`, bound to the preceding button using `onAction="#back"`:

```
@FXML
private void back(ActionEvent event) throws IOException {
        navigate(event, FXMLPage.LIST.getPage());
}
```

You may be wondering what the `FXMLPage.java` class does. It is an enum (for more about enums, visit `https://docs.oracle.com/javase/tutorial/java/javaOO/enum.html`). I have created enums to define all our FXML document names and their locations, in addition to any utility methods relevant to those FXML document, helping to ease coding in our system.

This concept of maintainability helps in large systems to maintain constant properties and functionality in one place for future ease of refactoring, and allows us to change names in one place instead of roaming all over the system to change just one name.

If you check system controllers, you will find all the logic for handling other button's actions – deleting, editing, clearing, and saving notes.

Power application change synchronization with properties

Properties are wrapper objects for JavaFX-based object attributes such as String or Integer. Properties allow you to add listener code to respond when the wrapped value of an object has changed or is flagged as invalid. In addition, property objects can be bound to one another.

Binding behavior allows properties to update or synchronize their values based on a changed value from another property.

Properties are wrapper objects that have the ability to make values accessible as read/writable or read-only.

In short, JavaFX's properties are wrapper objects holding actual values while providing change support, invalidation support, and binding capabilities. I will address binding later, but for now, let's examine the commonly used property classes.

All wrapper property classes are located in the `javafx.beans.property.*` package namespace. Listed here are the commonly used property classes. To see all of the property classes, refer to the documentation in Javadoc (`https://docs.oracle.com/javase/8/javafx/api/index.html?javafx/beans/property.html`).

- `javafx.beans.property.SimpleBooleanProperty`
- `javafx.beans.property.ReadOnlyBooleanWrapper`
- `javafx.beans.property.SimpleIntegerProperty`
- `javafx.beans.property.ReadOnlyIntegerWrapper`
- `javafx.beans.property.SimpleDoubleProperty`
- `javafx.beans.property.ReadOnlyDoubleWrapper`
- `javafx.beans.property.SimpleStringProperty`
- `javafx.beans.property.ReadOnlyStringWrapper`

The properties that have a prefix of `Simple` and a suffix of `Property` are the *read/writable property* classes, and the classes with a prefix of ReadOnly and a suffix of Wrapper are the read-only properties. Later, you will see how to create a JavaFX bean using these commonly used properties.

Let's fast-forward to JavaFX's Properties API to see how it handles the common issues. You may notice that the TableView control has been added to the main page to list the currently loaded notes and any new added notes.

In order to populate TableView correctly with data, we should have a data model to represent the notes data, and this is the first place I used the Properties API in the JavaFX JavaBean-style Note class, which is defined as the following:

```
public class Note {
    private final SimpleStringProperty title;
    private final SimpleStringProperty description;
    public Note(String title, String description) {
        this.title = new SimpleStringProperty(title);
        this.description = new SimpleStringProperty(description);
    }
    public String getTitle() {
        return title.get();
    }
    public void setTitle(String title) {
        this.title.set(title);
    }
    public String getDescription() {
        return description.get();
    }
    public void setDescription(String description) {
        this.description.set(description);
    }
}
```

In order to populate the TableView class with data already stored in the application database, for example (our database here is transient using ObservableList<Note> of the note object called data), we have to pass a collection of this data.

We need to remove the burden of updating the UI control (in our case, the TableView control) manually each time the notes data collection get updated. Therefore, we need a solution to automatically synchronize the changes between the table view and notes data collection model, for example, adding, updating, or deleting data, without any further modification to the UI controls from the code. Only the data model collection gets updated – the UI should be synchronized automatically.

This feature is already an integral part of JavaFX collections. We will use JavaFX's `ObservableList` class. The `ObservableList` class is a collection that is capable of notifying UI controls when objects are added, updated, or removed.

JavaFX's `ObservableList` class is typically used in list UI controls, such as `ListView` and `TableView`. Let's look at how we will use the `ObservableList` collection class.

In `BaseController`, I have created static data as `ObservableList<Note>` to be shared between all controllers, to be able to add, update, and remove notes from it. Also, it is initialized with some data as follows:

```
protected static ObservableList<Note> data =
  FXCollections.<Note>observableArrayList(
  new Note("Note 1", "Description of note 41"),
    new Note("Note 2", "Description of note 32"),
    new Note("Note 3", "Description of note 23"),
    new Note("Note 4", "Description of note 14"));
```

In the `ListNotesUIController.java` class, inside the `initialize()` method, I have created an instance of the `javafx.collections.transformation.FilteredList` class that will be used as the filtering class when we search in the table contents. It will pass the `data` object of type `ObservableList<Note>` as the source data:

```
FilteredList<Note> filteredData = new FilteredList<>
  (data, n -> true);
```

The second argument of `FilteredList` is the predicate used to filter data; here, it returns `true`, meaning no filtration, and we will add the filtration predicate later on.

The created data list of type `ObservableList<Note>` should be passed to our `TableView` data in order for the table view to monitor the current data collection manipulations, such as addition, deletion, editing, and filtering, as the following in the `initialize()` method of the `ListNotesUIController.java` class, but instead we have passed the `filteredData` wrapper instance:

```
notesListTable.setItems(filteredData);
```

The final step is to acknowledge our `notesListTable` columns, of type `TableColumn`, and to which property of Note class to render and take care of. We use the `setCellValueFactory()` method to do the trick, as shown here:

```
titleTc.setCellValueFactory(new PropertyValueFactory<>("title"));
descriptionTc.setCellValueFactory(new
PropertyValueFactory<>("description"));
```

Note that `title` and `description` are the instance variable names of the `Note` class.

Check the final project code for the full implementation. Then, run the application from the NetBeans main menu, choose Run, and then click on **Run Main Project**.

Try to add a new note and watch the table view for your newly added note. Try to select and delete the note or update an existing note. You will notice the change immediately.

By checking the application code, you will see that all we have done is manipulated the data list and all the other synchronization work efforts are carried out with the help of the `ObservableList` class.

Filtering the TableView data list

We will get in touch here with two of the most powerful Java SE 8 and JavaFX 8 features `Predicate` and `FilteredList`. Let's state the problem we have at hand and how we are going to solve it with the `stream` feature.

In our `ListNotesUI.fxml` page, you may notice the text field located above the notes table; its purpose here is to filter the current table data to narrow the result to get a specific note. Also, we need to maintain the current list being careful not to remove any data from it or query the database for each search hit.

We already have the notes data list and we are going to use the text field to filter this list for any note title or description containing this character or a combination of characters, as shown here:

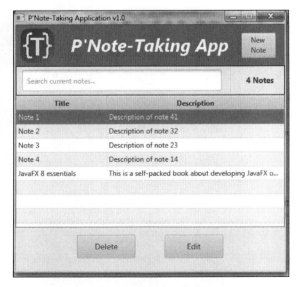

Table populated with data

Now, after typing in d, de, dev, or developing, JavaFX, a table will be filtered, as seen in the following screenshot. Also, try to remove all the text; you will find that the data comes back again. Next, we will discover how we did that.

Table data filtered with text in the search field

The following is the magical piece of code that did that:

```
searchNotes.setOnKeyReleased(e ->
{
  filteredData.setPredicate(n ->
  {
if (searchNotes.getText() == null || searchNotes.getText().isEmpty())
return true;

return n.getTitle().contains(searchNotes.getText())
|| n.getDescription().contains(searchNotes.getText());
  });
});
```

The `searchNotes` is a reference to the text field we are using to filter the notes data. We have registered it with a `setOnKeyReleased(EventHandler<? super KeyEvent> value)` method that gets our text to filter once any character is typed in. Also, note that we used the Lambda expression here to make the code more concise and clean.

Inside the definition of the action method, `filteredData` is a `FilteredList<Note>` class, we have passed a predicate `test()` method implementation to `setPredicate(Predicate<? super E> predicate)` filter only the notes title or a description matching the `searchNotes` text input.

The filtered data is automatically updated to the table UI.

For more information about the Predicate API, visit `http://docs.oracle.com/javase/8/docs/api/java/util/function/Predicate.html`.

Note-taking as a desktop application

Once you have finished the application, it will be more professional to not distribute the final jar and instead ask the user to install the JRE environment to be able to run your application, especially if you targeting a large audience.

It's more professional to prepare your native installer packages as `.exe`, `.msi`, `.dmg`. or `.img`.

Every installer manages the application requirements from the required assets and runtime environments. This ensures that your application will run on multiple platforms too.

Deploying the application for desktop distribution

One of the advanced NetBeans features is to allow you to bundle your application for different platforms via its deployment handler, which gives you the following main features:

- Deploy your application through native installers
- Manage application assets as application icons, splash screens, and native installer icons
- Accept the certificate for the final signing of your application when preparing the final package

- Manage the required JavaFX runtime version
- Adding desktop shortcuts of the Start menu when using Windows
- Handling the Java Web Start technology requirements and customizations

Let's see the configuration of NetBeans deployment:

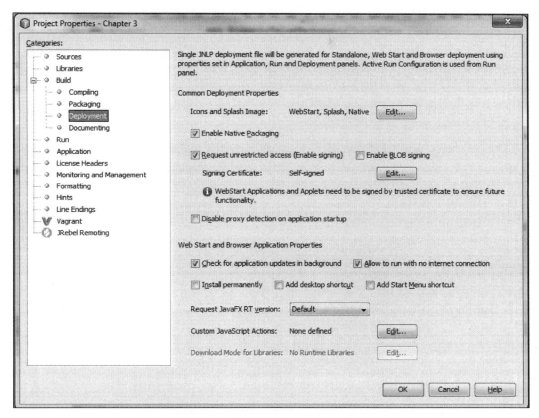

NetBeans deployment configurations

To know how to package your application into the native installer for each platform you are targeting, visit the following URL, which provides you with all the required steps and software to complete the task:

```
https://netbeans.org/kb/docs/java/native_pkg.html
```

JavaFX on the Web

In this section, we will learn about JavaFX on the Web and how to deploy our note-taking application there.

WebEngine

JavaFX provides a non-GUI component capable of loading HTML5 content, called the **WebEngine** API (`javafx.scene.web.WebEngine`). This API is basically an object instance of the `WebEngine` class to be used to load a file containing HTML5 content. The HTML5 file could be loaded from a local file system, a web server, or from inside a JAR file.

When a file is loaded using a web engine object, a background thread is used to load the file content to not block the *JavaFX application thread*.

The following are two `WebEngine` methods for loading HTML5 content:

* load(String URL)
* loadContent(String HTML)

WebView

JavaFX provides a GUI `WebView` (`javafx.scene.web.WebView`) node that can render HTML5 content onto the Scene graph. A `WebView` node is basically a mini-browser that is capable of responding to web events and allows a developer to interact with the HTML5 content.

Because of the close relationship between loading web content and the ability to display web content, the `WebView` node object also contains a `WebEngine` instance.

The JavaFX 8 `WebView` class implementation provides support for the following HTML5 features:

* Canvas and SVG
* Media playback
* Form controls
* History maintenance
* Interactive element tags

- DOM
- Web workers
- Web sockets
- Web fonts

WebView and engine in action

We are going to have a simple example of how to load an HTML5 web document that contains Google Maps integrated with JavaFX as the scene control using `WebView`. We then use `WebEngine` to get the longitude and latitude from the JavaFX `TextField` controls to execute a JavaScript method that passes those parameters to position the map to be centered to the newly passed position with the marker indication, as shown in the following figure:

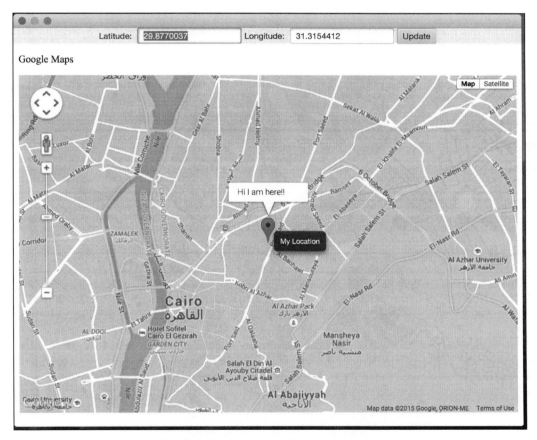

The Google Maps viewer from the JavaFX 8 application

For the sake of clarity, I will show and explain only the important parts of the code, which demonstrates the concept mentioned in the preceding paragraph. For the complete code in this chapter, check the web package code GoogleMapViewerFX. java class and map.html file.

To view Google Maps inside the JavaFX application, we need to first create an HTML file to load and integrate with the Maps API, and this is defined in the map.html file. As seen in the preceding picture, the location is centered on Cairo, Egypt, my city, and this is set as the longitude and latitude values passed to the map when we create it, as in the following code snippet:

```
var latlng = new google.maps.LatLng(30.0594885, 31.2584644);
var Options = {
    zoom: 13,
    center: latlng,
    mapTypeId: google.maps.MapTypeId.ROADMAP
};
var map = new google.maps.Map(document.getElementById("canvas"),
  Options);
```

Next, we have to notice the JavaScript goToLocation(lng, lat) method; this will be called from the JavaFX application using the webEngine instance to position the map based on the passed longitude and latitude from the JavaFX controls.

Inside GoogleMapViewerFX.java, we have created four controls to compose our UI – two TextField classes for the longitude and latitude, one update button, and a WebView object to view the map.html document:

```
WebView webView = new WebView();
WebEngine webEngine = webView.getEngine();
final TextField latitude = new TextField("" + 29.8770037);
final TextField longitude = new TextField("" + 31.3154412);
Button update = new Button("Update");
```

Note that I have created text controls with the initial longitude and latitude, which is different from the original map position. This position is my home position, and you can change it to yours and hit update to view the new position.

To load the map.html file, we have to pass it to the WebEngine class that we created from the WebView class we have created already, as seen in the previous code snippet.

Implement the button's `onAction()` method to allow integration between JavaFX controls and JavaScript using the `webEngine executeScript()` method, as in the following code:

```
update.setOnAction(evt -> {
    double lat = Double.parseDouble(latitude.getText());
    double lon = Double.parseDouble(longitude.getText());

    webEngine.executeScript("" +
            "window.lat = " + lat + ";" +
            "window.lon = " + lon + ";" +
            "document.goToLocation(window.lat, window.lon);");
});
```

Run the application and you should see the previous figure positioned to Cairo city! Hit update and you should reach my home, as seen in the following figure.

Try getting your position longitude and latitude; then go to your home too!

Powerful, isn't it? It is very easy to integrate HTML5 content and interact with already developed web applications to add more rich content from the Web to your existing JavaFX application.

Change the Google Map position in the JavaFX 8 application

Note-taking as a web application

Once your application is tested, as we have discussed before, you can distribute your application to multiple platforms and environments. We did that already for desktops with native installers using the distributed in this chapter, `.jar` file under the project's `dist` folder.

The same `.jar` file will be used for web deployment, and the application could be deployed as a web application in many ways, as we will see next.

Running the application for the Web

There are three ways to run your JavaFX application on the Web:

1. Using **Java Web Start** to download and start your application once; then, you can use it offline from your machine

2. Embed your JAR into your HTML file to run from an enterprise environment

3. Load your HTML content from the `WebEngine` class and view it from the `WebView` class, as discussed previously

Java Web Start

The Java Web Start software provides the power to launch full-featured applications with a single click. Users can download and launch applications, such as a complete spreadsheet program or an Internet chat client, without going through lengthy installation procedures.

With Java Web Start, users can launch a Java application by clicking on a link on a web page. The link points to a **JNLP** (**Java Network Launch Protocol**) file, which instructs Java Web Start to download, cache, and run the application.

Java Web Start provides Java developers and users with many deployment advantages:

- With Java Web Start, you can place a single Java application on a web server for deployment to a wide variety of platforms, including Windows, Linux, and Solaris.

- It supports multiple simultaneous versions of the Java platform. An application can request a specific version of the Java Runtime Environment (JRE) software without conflicting with the needs of other applications.

- Users can create a desktop shortcut to launch a Java Web Start application outside a browser.

- Java Web Start takes advantage of the inherent security of the Java platform. By default, applications have restricted access to local disk and network resources.

- Applications launched with Java Web Start are cached locally for improved performance.

- Updates to a Java Web Start application are automatically downloaded when the application is run standalone from the user's desktop.

Java Web Start is installed as part of the JRE software. Users do not have to install Java Web Start separately or perform additional tasks to use Java Web Start applications.

For more information about **Java Web Start,** see the following links:

- Java Web Start Guide (`http://docs.oracle.com/javase/8/docs/technotes/guides/javaws/developersguide/contents.html`)

- The `javax.jnlp` API Documentation (`http://docs.oracle.com/javase/8/docs/jre/api/javaws/jnlp/index.html`)

- The Java Web Start Developers Site (`http://www.oracle.com/technetwork/java/javase/javawebstart/index.html`)

Deploying the application for a web distribution

To deploy your JavaFX applications on to the Web, there is a very simple way using NetBeans.

NetBeans already provides three deployment types for your JavaFX application – desktop, Java Web Start, and Web-as seen in the following figure:

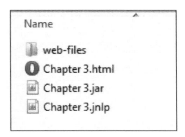

Summary

So far, we have been learning how to develop JavaFX enterprise applications for both desktops and the Web.

In this chapter, we gained the skills to develop any application, starting with sketching a layout on a piece of paper; next, we translated it into an actual interactive, colorful UI prototype. We saw how to nest our containers and controls to achieve the desired layout. Once we got the approvals for final development, we brought the application to life by making it respond to customer actions and by delivering the functional requirements.

We made our code more powerful, clean, and concise with the power of Java SE 8 features and JavaFX bindings. Finally, we learned how to deploy our application either to the target desktop customers or Web users for different platforms and environments.

In the next chapter, we are going to learn how to develop a JavaFX application for Android-based smart phones. Additionally, we will learn the required skills to download and install Android SDK tools and interact with loggers, emulators, and other tools that will help you in any future mobile development you need to do that isn't related to JavaFX.

4
Developing a JavaFX Application for Android

There is no doubt that we are seeing a rise in non-PC clients every day. Almost everyone has at least one mobile phone or tablet, maybe from different vendors, but certainly with Android or iOS, given that they represent 96 percent of smart phone OSs sold in 2014.

Smart phones and tablets are extremely popular nowadays and these figures are increasing every year. And that is why developers should consider gaining the skills required to develop applications for such a great market.

JavaFX 8 already delivers rich client applications for Web and desktop, as we have seen in *Chapter 3, Developing a JavaFX Desktop and Web Application*. But, like me, if you have written a JavaFX application, you definitely want it to run on as many devices as possible to follow the true spirit of *Write Once, Run Anywhere*. I would like to take this opportunity to inform you that, yes, we can run JavaFX on mobile devices.

Based on the official support from Oracle Corporation for JavaFX, a number of people inside the JavaFX community are working to port JavaFX to make it run on as many devices and platforms as possible (desktop, mobile, and embedded) and different operating systems, with the same codebase.

They have successfully created SDKs that allow us to develop JavaFX applications as native applications to run on Android or iOS-based devices in one bundle (*JVM plus application*) without any extra software needed to run them as in desktop or Web.

This chapter will give you the essential hands-on knowledge about SDKs that will allow you to create, package, and deploy native applications for Android.

Here are some skills that will be gained during this chapter:

- Installing and configuring Android environment tools and software
- Preparing and creating the JavaFX 8 mobile project structure
- Creating an Android JavaFX 8 application
- Interoperability between JavaFX 8 and Android low-level APIs
- Packaging and deploying applications on mobile devices
- Signing the application for final Google Play Store submission

Why port JavaFX into the mobile environment?

Why port JavaFX into the mobile environment? Isn't it **Write Once Run Anywhere (WORA)**? This is a very good question to ask. Any Java application follows the WORA paradigm, but with a very critical abstract piece of software that it relies on to run and is called **Java Virtual Machine (JVM)**.

JVM is the software responsible for translating the compiled byte code (*.class file*) for a specific machine and providing platform instructions that it can understand and run, so you can run your application. Therefore, you will find different versions of JRE or **JDK** for each hardware (Intel, AMD, SPARC, or ARM) and platform (Windows, Mac, Linux, or Solaris).

On Desktop, Web, or embedded devices, you have to first install the **Java Runtime Environment (JRE)** to be able to run your Java application. But, for mobile devices, you will notice that you just download your application from the Store, install it, and finally run it without any extra software. Also, some closed platforms don't allow the JVM to be installed.

For a better end user experience, there should be no difference between running JavaFX applications and running other applications targeting Android or iOS.

Therefore, we should have a self-contained (the application plus JVM) JavaFX application that can run on mobile devices. In addition to the ability to interact with Android low-level APIs to control device features, it will be treated similarly to other applications in the Google Play Store.

We should thank the community for bringing up such porting SDKs and filling this gap to allow us to create and run our JavaFX applications on iOS using the port from RoboVM (`http://www.robovm.org/`) and on Android using the port from JavaFXPorts (`http://javafxports.org/`).

Since February 2015, an agreement between the companies behind those projects has been in force, and now a single plugin called `jfxmobile-plugin` allows us to build applications for three platforms desktop, Android, and iOS from the same codebase.

Also, a new company called **Gluon** offers a free plugin (`http://gluonhq.com/products/tools/ide-plugins/`) for **NetBeans** that creates a project with everything required to build applications based on `jfxmobile-plugin`.

 But bear in mind that all of this is constantly evolving and things may change from what is stated here.

How it works

Both RoboVM for iOS porting and JavaFXPorts for Android porting contain all the required libraries to make it easy to package your JavaFX 8 application with the required runtime environment.

When using RoboVM for iOS to package your JavaFX application (to an `.ipa` package file), all your JavaFX applications are transformed into **Objective-C** (currently **Swift**) applications.

When packaging your JavaFX application using JavaFXPorts for Android (to the `.apk` package file), the applications are transformed into Android packages running on top of the **Dalvik** VM.

These SDKs contain a lot of native code that will be ported to iOS and Android after injecting them inside your JavaFX application in order to increase application performance.

Using these SDK's, we can package our applications into formats (`.ipa` for iOS and `.apk` for Android) that are suitable for submission to Stores.

Who is maintaining it?

Don't worry—there is free support on a large scale for porting JavaFX to both Android and iOS, as well as commercial support.

 For free and commercial support, both the RoboVM and JavaFXPorts communities use this Google group:

https://groups.google.com/forum/#!forum/javafxports

Free and commercial support is mainly available from people in the community and those who are actively involved in both projects. And they encourage more third parties to be involved as well.

For iOS, RoboVM has different plans for developers; you can check them at http://robovm.com/pricing/.

While for Android, the company **LodgON** offers support for JavaFX-Android integration as part of their support for JavaFX porting (http://www.lodgon.com/dali/page/JavaFX_Consulting).

Getting started

We now have enough information on how the tools and SDKs discussed previously will let us get started on developing our JavaFX applications and porting them to Android mobile devices.

But before moving to the development stage, we should have the tools and software installed and configured properly in order to complete the development process, based on the provided SDKs, to have a final .apk package at hand.

We will deploy this .apk package on real devices and finally we will sign it for final submission to Google Play Store.

So let's get started with installing the prerequisite tools and software to start developing our application.

Preparing and installing the prerequisite software

We need to install the following list of tools and software in order to have our build process complete without any problem.

Java SE 8 JDK8 u45

We have already done this before; refer to the *Installing Java SE 8 JDK* section in *Chapter 1, Getting Started with JavaFX 8*.

> Java SE 8 update 40 is the minimum version required in order to develop JavaFX applications for Android.

Gradle

From their website, this is the definition of Gradle:

> *Gradle is an open source build automation system. Gradle can automate the building, testing, publishing, deployment, and more of software packages or other types of projects, such as generated static websites, generated documentation, or indeed anything else.*

Recently, Android development tools changed their build system to Gradle. The RoboVM and JavaFXPorts porting projects mimic the same tools.

Installing Gradle is a very straightforward task:

1. Go to `https://gradle.org`.

2. From the right-hand side, under the **GET GRADLE!** Section, click on **Downloads 2.4** (as of this writing) and the download process will start for the `gradle-2.4-all.zip` file.

3. Copy the downloaded `.zip` file into a convenient location of your choice and unzip it.

4. The final step is to set the environment variable into your system as the following:

   ° On Windows – Assume Gradle is installed at `c:\tools\gradle_2.4`:

   ```
   set GRADLE_HOME=c:\tools\gradle_2.4
   set PATH=%PATH%;%GRADLE_HOME%\bin
   ```

   ° On Mac – Assume Gradle is installed at `/usr/local/tools/gradle_2.4`:

   ```
   export GRADLE_HOME=/usr/local/tools/gradle_2.4
   export PATH=${PATH}:${GRADLE_HOME}/bin
   ```

Android SDK

The Android SDK includes the complete set of development and debugging tools for the Android platform.

Installing Android SDK is a very straightforward task:

1. Go to `http://developer.android.com/sdk/index.html#Other`.

2. Under SDK Tools Only, click on `android-sdk_r24.2-{platform}`. `{exe|zip|tgz}` (as of this writing) against the name of your favorite platform:

Platform	Package	Size	SHA-1 Checksum
Windows	installer_r24.2-windows.exe (Recommended)	107849819 bytes	e764ea93aa72766737f9be3b9fb3e42d879ab599
	android-sdk_r24.2-windows.zip	155944165 bytes	2611ed9a6080f4838f1d4e55172801714a8a169b
Mac OS X	android-sdk_r24.2-macosx.zip	88949635 bytes	256c9bf642f56242d963c090d147de7402733451
Linux	android-sdk_r24.2-linux.tgz	168119905 bytes	1a29f9827ef395a96db629209b0e38d5e2dd8089

3. A `Download` page will open; accept the terms, click on the `Download` `android-sdk_r24.2-{platform}.{exe|zip|tgz}` button, and the download process will start.

4. Copy the downloaded `.zip` file into a convenient location and unzip it, or double-click the `.exe` on Windows to start the installation.

5. From the command line, run the following:

```
$ android
```

The Android SDK Manager will open; click on `Build-tools version` `21.1.2` or higher and the SDK Platform for API 21 or higher.

Click on **Install x packages**, accept the license, and click on **Install**. You are done.

A good reference for Android SDK Manager is at `http://developer.` `android.com/sdk/installing/adding-packages.html`.

6. The final step is to set the environment variable in your system as follows:

- On Windows – Assume the Android SDK is installed at `c:\tools\android_ADT`:

  ```
  set ANDROID_HOME=c:\tools\android_ADT\sdk

  set PATH=%PATH%;%ANDROID_HOME%\platform-tools;%ANDROID_HOME%\tools
  ```

- On Mac – Assume the Android SDK is installed at `/usr/local/tools/android_ADT`:

  ```
  export ANDROID_HOME=/usr/local/tools/android_adt/sdk

  export PATH=${PATH}:${ANDROID_HOME}/tools:${ANDROID_HOME}/platform-tools
  ```

- The best approach for this is to create a Gradle property with the name ANDROID_HOME defined under `C:\Users\<user>\.gradle\gradle.properties`

Preparing the project for Android

We have successfully installed the prerequisite software and tools and configured the environmental variables, so we are ready to start developing the application that will be ported into the Android device.

But before we do so, we need to prepare our project structure and the build file as well in order to be ready for building and packaging our application with JavaFXPorts libraries.

Setting up a complex project with three different platforms would have been a hard task, until now. But recently, Gluon (http://gluonhq.com/) has released a NetBeans plugin (`http://gluonhq.com/gluon-plugin-for-netbeans/`) that simplifies this task to a great degree.

Project structure

The easiest way is to use the Gluon plugin for NetBeans. This will create everything for you a Java project, where you just need to add the JavaFX sources, and a `build.gradle` file with all the tasks ready.

Once you have installed the plugin, perform the following tasks:

1. Just create a new JavaFX project and select **Basic Gluon Application**, as shown here:

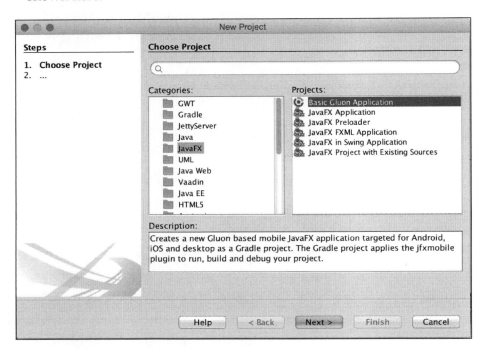

2. Select valid names for the project (DialPad2), packages (packt.taman.jfx8. ch4), and the main class (DialPad2) and you will find a bunch of folders in your new project.

3. The top project structure following the Gluon plugin will bring a more complex structure and should be as seen in the following screenshot:

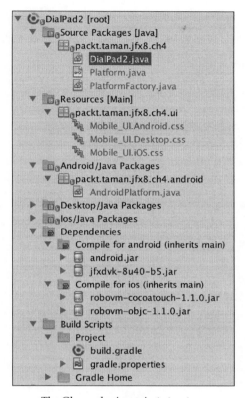

The Gluon plugin project structure

Next, we are going to add our build script file to complete our mission.

Using Gradle

To build a Gradle project, we need the `build.gradle` script file. The Gluon plugin has already added this file for you by default, including all the properties to allow our application to run and compile successfully.

The default Gradle build file created `build.gradle` file should be as follows:

```
buildscript {
    repositories {
        jcenter()
    }
    dependencies {
        classpath 'org.javafxports:jfxmobile-plugin:1.0.0-b8'
    }
}

apply plugin: 'org.javafxports.jfxmobile'

repositories {
    jcenter()
}

mainClassName = 'packt.taman.jfx8.ch4.DialPad2'

jfxmobile {

    android {
        manifest = 'lib/android/AndroidManifest.xml'
    }
}
```

The only important thing to change is the `jfxmobile-plugin` version to 1.0.0-b8 (or the most recent one; check `https://bitbucket.org/javafxports/javafxmobile-plugin/overview` frequently to keep it updated).

The application

The fact that you have reached this section means that we have finished setting up the application project structure correctly, and it's now ready for mobile device development.

Our application will be a new smart phone dial pad interface to perform calls on our device with its default dialer. It will be customized with CSS to control its skinning style, which can be modified to get the native look and feel for different platforms.

The main aim of this application is to provide a new UI concept (to customize an application using CSS), and you will learn how to use the CSS id and class selectors as well as setting them from inside the code to be applied to different controls.

The following screenshots show the application before and after applying the CSS file:

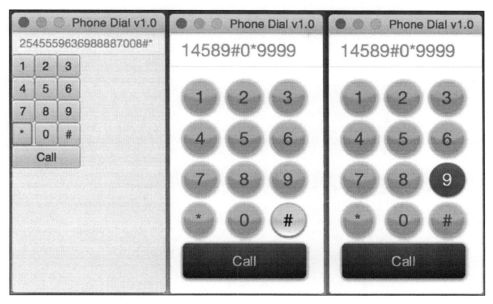

| Before applying CSS | After applying CSS | Key pressed |

Developing and styling an application UI with CSS

As we have learned before, I will start prototyping our application; after the prototyping, we should have the application UI we saw earlier.

This application UI is written directly inside the `start(Stage)` function of the class `DialPad2.java`, as an alternative way to develop UIs rather than using static FXML design.

Here, we nested controls from inside the code in case we need to dynamically generate UI controls and assign them different settings, CSS classes, ids selectors, and listeners.

The following code snippet shows how we produced the preceding application UI:

```java
BorderPane root = new BorderPane();
Rectangle2D bounds = Screen.getPrimary().getVisualBounds();
Scene scene = new Scene(root, bounds.getWidth(),
  bounds.getHeight());
scene.getStylesheets().add(getClass().getResource("ui/Mobile_UI."+
  PlatformFactory.getName()+".css").toExternalForm());
TextField output = new TextField("");
output.setDisable(true);

root.setTop(output);
String[] keys = {"1", "2", "3",
                 "4", "5", "6",
                 "7", "8", "9",
                 "*", "0", "#"};

GridPane numPad = new GridPane();
numPad.setAlignment(Pos.CENTER);
numPad.getStyleClass().add("num-pad");
for (int i = 0; i < keys.length; i++) {
     Button button = new Button(keys[i]);
     button.getStyleClass().add("dial-num-btn");
     button.setOnAction(e ->
        output.setText(output.getText().concat(Button.class.
     cast(e.getSource()).getText())));
     numPad.add(button, i % 3, (int) Math.ceil(i / 3));
}
// Call button
Button call = new Button("Call");
call.setOnAction(e->PlatformFactory.getPlatform().
  callNumber(output.getText()));
call.setId("call-btn");
call.setMaxSize(Double.MAX_VALUE, Double.MAX_VALUE);
numPad.add(call, 0, 4);
GridPane.setColumnSpan(call, 3);
GridPane.setHgrow(call, Priority.ALWAYS);
root.setCenter(numPad);

//Stage setup
stage.setScene(scene);
stage.setTitle("Phone Dial v2.0");
stage.show();
```

The code starts by creating a scene that has `BorderPane` as a root node. After the scene is created, the code loads the CSS style sheet file, `Mobile_UI.<platform>.css`, to style the current scene's nodes via the `getStylesheets().add()` method as follows:

```
scene.getStylesheets().add(getClass().getResource("ui/Mobile_
UI."+PlatformFactory.getName()+".css").toExternalForm());
```

After we have created a `TextField` output to show the dial result and set it to be disabled so we can't edit it, the numbers are added and displayed just by clicking on the buttons.

Next, the code simply creates a grid using the `GridPane` class and generates 12 buttons to be placed in each cell. Notice in the for loop that each button is set with the style class named `dial-num-btn` via the `getStyleClass().add()` method.

 We use here an old classic `for` loop for adding the buttons, and not a fancy Java 8 stream. Be aware that `Dalvik VM` runs only on Java 7, and only lambdas can be used (since, internally, JavaFXPorts uses the Retrolambda project).

Lastly, the dark blue **Call** button will be added to the last row of the grid pane. Because the **Call** button is unique, its id selector is set with `#call-btn`, and it will be styled using the id selector, which means the selector named inside the CSS file will be prefixed with the # symbol.

The following is the CSS file used to style the application:

```
.root {
    -fx-background-color: white;
    -fx-font-size: 20px;
    bright-green: rgb(59,223, 86);
    bluish-gray: rgb(189,218,230);
}
.num-pad {
    -fx-padding: 15px, 15px, 15px, 15px;
    -fx-hgap: 10px;
    -fx-vgap: 8px;
}

#call-btn {
    -fx-background-color:
        #090a0c,
```

```
        linear-gradient(#38424b 0%, #1f2429 20%, #191d22 100%),
        linear-gradient(#20262b, #191d22),
        radial-gradient(center 50% 0%, radius 100%,
            rgba(114,131,148,0.9), rgba(255,255,255,0));
    -fx-background-radius: 5,4,3,5;
    -fx-background-insets: 0,1,2,0;
    -fx-text-fill: white;
    -fx-effect: dropshadow( three-pass-box , rgba(0,0,0,0.6) , 5,
        0.0 , 0 , 1 );
    -fx-font-family: "Arial";
    -fx-text-fill: linear-gradient(white, #d0d0d0);
    -fx-font-size: 16px;
    -fx-padding: 10 20 10 20;
}
#call-btn .text {
    -fx-effect: dropshadow( one-pass-box , rgba(0,0,0,0.9) , 1,
        0.0 , 0 , 1 );
}


.dial-num-btn {
    -fx-background-color:
        linear-gradient(#f0ff35, #a9ff00),
        radial-gradient(center 50% -40%, radius 200%, #b8ee36 45%,
            #80c800 50%);
    -fx-background-radius: 30;
    -fx-background-insets: 0,1,1;
    -fx-effect: dropshadow( three-pass-box , rgba(0,0,0,0.4) , 5,
        0.0 , 0 , 1 );
    -fx-text-fill: #395306;
}


.dial-num-btn:hover {
    -fx-background-color:
        #c3c4c4,
        linear-gradient(#d6d6d6 50%, white 100%),
        radial-gradient(center 50% -40%, radius 200%, #e6e6e6 45%,
            rgba(230,230,230,0) 50%);
    -fx-background-radius: 30;
    -fx-background-insets: 0,1,1;
    -fx-text-fill: black;
    -fx-effect: dropshadow( three-pass-box , rgba(0,0,0,0.6) , 3,
        0.0 , 0 , 1 );
}
```

```css
.dial-num-btn:pressed {
    -fx-background-color: linear-gradient(#ff5400, #be1d00);
    -fx-background-radius: 30;
    -fx-background-insets: 0,1,1;
    -fx-text-fill: white;
}
```

For more information about JavaFX 8 CSS properties, visit the following JavaFX 8 CSS reference:

```
http://docs.oracle.com/javase/8/javafx/api/javafx/scene/doc-files/
cssref.html
```

Adding some logic

As you have seen in the code snippet, each of the 12 buttons has an action assigned using a lambda expression that is dynamically created as follows:

```
button.setOnAction(e -> output.setText(output.getText().
    concat(Button.class.cast(e.getSource()).getText())));
```

We get the output `TextField` and concatenate the next number, asterisk, or hash symbol by getting the source of the event `e`, which in our case is the clicked button, and then its text value, containing the number to dial.

Making your project ready for mobile devices

Basically, this new project was generated with the Gluon plugin (`build.gradle` updated to **b8**).

In order to make the application ready for mobile devices, we need to adjust its height and width to the target device screen and make the UI tree respond to that accordingly.

This is a very simple yet important step and we can adjust the following line of code by setting the scene height and width to the target device screen dimensions dynamically. Have a look at the following line:

```
Scene scene = new Scene(root, 175, 300);
```

Change this to the following lines of code:

```
Rectangle2D bounds = Screen.getPrimary().getVisualBounds();
Scene scene = new Scene(root, bounds.getWidth(),
    bounds.getHeight());
```

The first line gets the device screen bounds. Then we set the scene height and width from this bounds variable.

The second line adds your sources to the Sources Packages [Java] and Resources [Main]. It then adds a PlatformFactory class, which is in charge of finding which platform the project is running from. Have a look at the Platform interface with a method signature:

```
public interface Platform {
    void callNumber(String number);
}
```

This allows you to call the following method on your source:

```
Button call = new Button("Call");
call.setOnAction(e->
PlatformFactory.getPlatform().callNumber(output.getText()));
```

Finally, you provide the native solution for each platform. For instance, for Android:

```
public class AndroidPlatform implements Platform {

    @Override
    public void callNumber(String number) {
        if (!number.equals("")) {
            Uri uriNumber = Uri.parse("tel:" + number);
            Intent dial = new Intent(Intent.ACTION_CALL,
                uriNumber);
            FXActivity.getInstance().startActivity(dial);
        }
    }
}
```

For this to work on Android, we only need to modify AndroidManifest.xml, adding the required permission and the activity intent. This custom manifest has to be referenced on the build.gradle file as follows:

```
android {
    manifest = 'lib/android/AndroidManifest.xml'
  }
```

Interoperability with low-level Android APIs

You need `android.jar` in order to use the Android API's, and you need `jfxdvk.jar` in order to access the `FXActivity` class, which is the bridge between `JavaFX` and the `Dalvik` runtime. We use a static method on the `FXActivity` to retrieve the `FXActivity`, which extends the Android `Context`. This `Context` can be used to look up Android services.

Building the application

In order to create our Android `.apk` package file for our application, we need to build our application first; it is a very easy task. With the command line (or from NetBeans, right-click on the **project** tab and select `Tasks/task`) pointing to the current project folder, run the following command:

```
$ gradle build
```

Gradle will download all the required libraries and start building our application. Once finished, you should see the successful output as follows:

```
$ gradle build
Download https://jcenter.bintray.com/org/robovm/robovm-rt/1.0.0-
beta-04/robovm-rt-1.0.0-beta-08.pom
:compileJava
:compileRetrolambdaMain
Download https://jcenter.bintray.com/net/orfjackal/retrolambda/
retrolambda/1.8.0/retrolambda-1.8.0.pom
:processResources UP-TO-DATE
:classes
:compileDesktopJava UP-TO-DATE
:compileRetrolambdaDesktop SKIPPED
........ . . ....
:check UP-TO-DATE
:build

BUILD SUCCESSFUL
Total time: 44.74 secs
```

Until now, we have built our application successfully. Next we need to generate the `.apk` and deploy it to many sources.

Building the final .apk Android package

We have two options when it comes to building our .apk file. The first is by running the following command:

```
gradle android
```

This will generate the .apk file in the directory build/javafxports/android.

The second is by running this command:

```
androidInstall
```

This will deploy the generated .apk package onto a device that is connected to your desktop or laptop device.

We will use the first option (gradle android) to make sure that we are able to generate the .apk file successfully. When done successfully, you should have a file named DialPad2.apk under the path mentioned previously.

Deploying the application

To be able to deploy our application on the connected mobile device using the gradle androidInstall command, you have to enable **Developer Options** and enable some other settings inside it on your device, as follows:

1. From your device, tap on **Settings** to open the setting menu.
2. From the top menu, choose **More**. The options depend on your device.
3. At the end of the **More Options** menu list, you should see **Developer Options**.
4. Tap on the **Developer Options** menu.
5. Enable **Developer Options** by turning on the slider at the top-right corner.
6. Under **debugging**, enable **USB debugging**, click on the **OK** button in the **Allow USB debugging** alert window, and enable **Unknown sources**.
7. Congratulations! You are done—let's go and install our application.

> **Optional**: if you don't see **Developer Options**, don't worry. It is present but hidden. Here is the magic—tap on **About device**, locate **Build number**, and tap on it 5 times (7 times on Lollipop). You will see a countdown of numbers, and at the end **Developer Options** will be enabled.

Deploying on Android-based devices

No as we are ready run the following command:

```
$ gradle androidinstall
```

After issuing this command, it will start building and packaging the JavaFX 8 application. The plugin will connect to your connected device and install the application into it. This is the result you should have:

```
:compileJava
:compileRetrolambdaMain
..........  .  .  ...
:processAndroidResources UP-TO-DATE
:apk
:zipalign
:androidInstall
Installed on device.

BUILD SUCCESSFUL
Total time: 47.537 secs
```

Now open your device and locate your applications icon from the home screen; in the bottom-right corner, you should see your `DialPad2` JavaFX application installed as seen in the following screenshot, with the default Android icon:

The JavaFX 8 application installed on the Android device

Tap the **DialPad2** application, and you should see your application up-and-running on your device and fully functional as intended:

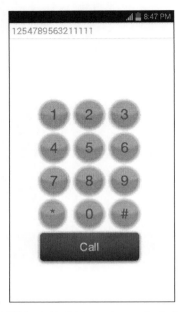

The JavaFX 8 application running on Android device

Tap the **Call** button and the Android default dialer will be launched, dialing the number you have typed in, as shown here:

The JavaFX 8 application dialing a number

If something doesn't work as expected, go to the command line and type in:

```
$ adb logcat
```

And you will have the output from all the applications on your device.

Deploying on the Google Play Store

In order to deploy your application on the Google Play Store, you have to perform the following:

1. You have to be enroll yourself with Google Play Developers (`https://play.google.com/apps/publish/`), fill a form with the description and several screenshots, and finally submit the DialPad2 apk.

2. In the `AndroidManifest.xml`, you have to disable the debugging option by adding `android:debuggable="false"` on the `application` tag.

3. You can also add the icon of your app (`android:icon="@icons/ic_launcher`) under the `application` tag. Here, `icons-*` are image folders with several resolutions.

Signing the APK

The `apk` must be signed for release. **Signed** means you need a private key; for that, we can use keytool (`http://developer.android.com/tools/publishing/app-signing.html#signing-manually`).

And **release** means that we need to add the signing configuration to `build.gradle` as follows:

```
jfxmobile {
    android {
        signingConfig {
            storeFile file("path/to/my-release-key.keystore")
            storePassword 'STORE_PASSWORD'
            keyAlias 'KEY_ALIAS'
            keyPassword 'KEY_PASSWORD'
        }
        manifest = 'lib/android/AndroidManifest.xml'
        resDirectory = 'src/android/resources'
    }
}
```

Right-click on the **DialPad2** project and, from **Tasks**, choose **apk** and then **apkRelease**.

Congratulations! The resulting `DialPad2.apk` is ready for submission to Google Play Store.

Testing tips

The most important point before delivering your application is to test it, especially on different Android based mobile devices.

In my experience with the mobile industry, I have found a dozen vendors' test mobile and tablets running the Android platform, each of them customizing the UI layer of each device with different capabilities and performance.

The four golden rules in the mobile testing field from my experience are:

1. Test on as many real devices and Android platforms as possible to cover all cases that your application will run on and to know how it will behave in production.

2. Use simulators only for *GUI testing and functionality* and not for *performance testing*. All simulators rely on your underlying PC/laptop hardware and memory, while on mobile hardware it will be quite different and very challenging to achieve the same performance.

3. There is a new simulator called ARC Welder for Chrome. Check it out at `https://developer.chrome.com/apps/getstarted_arc`.

4. Test on real devices for final production and performance testing. This is so you are assured that your application will act accordingly on the targeted market devices.

Summary

This chapter gave you a very good understanding of the mobile industry and how JavaFX-based applications can be developed and customized using different projects such as **RoboVM** for **iOS** and **JavaFXPorts** for **Android** to make it possible to run your application on both platforms.

We then learned how to install the required software and tools for Android development and to enable Android SDK along with *JavaFXPorts* libraries to package and install our dialer JavaFX-based application on a real Android device and submit it to Google Play Store.

We saw how to customize our application using CSS to have a different look and feel for the same application to make sure you have provided a different CSS for the Android version.

Next, we learned how to enable our device in the debugging mode to successfully install the application from jfxmobile-plugin via the command line. Finally, we covered the four golden rules of testing.

The next chapter will not differ too much from this one, but will give you a very good introduction to, and knowledge of, targeting your JavaFX 8 application to run on iOS-based devices. You will also learn how to use its development tools.

5
Developing a JavaFX Application for iOS

Apple has a great market share in the mobile and PC/Laptop world, with many different devices, from mobile phones such as the iPhone to musical devices such as the iPod and tablets such as the iPad.

It has a rapidly growing application market, called the Apple Store, serving its community, where the number of available apps increases daily. Mobile application developers should be ready for such a market.

Mobile application developers targeting both iOS and Android face many challenges. By just comparing the native development environments of these two platforms, you will find that they differ substantially.

iOS development, according to Apple, is based on the **Xcode IDE** (`https://developer.apple.com/xcode/`) and its programming languages. Traditionally, it was **Objetive-C** and, in June 2014, Apple introduced **Swift** (`https://developer.apple.com/swift/`); on the other hand, *Android* development, as defined by Google, is based on the Intellij IDEA IDE and the Java programming language.

Not many developers are proficient in both environments. In addition, these differences rule out any code reuse between the platforms.

JavaFX 8 is filling the gap for reusable code between the platforms, as we will see in this chapter, by sharing the same application in both platforms.

Here are some skills that you will have gained by the end of this chapter:

- Installing and configuring iOS environment tools and software
- Creating iOS JavaFX 8 applications
- Simulating and debugging JavaFX mobile applications
- Packaging and deploying applications on iOS mobile devices

Using RoboVM to run JavaFX on iOS

RoboVM is the bridge from Java to Objetive-C. Using this, it becomes easy to develop JavaFX 8 applications that are to be run on iOS-based devices, as the ultimate goal of the **RoboVM** project is to solve this problem without compromising on developer experience or app user experience.

As we saw in the previous chapter about Android, using *JavaFXPorts* to generate APKs was a relatively easy task due to the fact that Android is based on Java and the **Dalvik VM**.

On the contrary, iOS doesn't have a VM for Java, and it doesn't allow dynamic loading of native libraries.

Another approach is required. The RoboVM open source project tries to close the gap for Java developers by creating a bridge between Java and Objective-C using an *ahead-of-time* compiler that translates Java bytecode into native ARM or x86 machine code.

Features

Let's go through the RoboVM features:

- Brings Java and other JVM languages, such as Scala, Clojure, and Groovy, to iOS-based devices
- Translates Java bytecode into machine code ahead of time for fast execution directly on the CPU without any overhead
- The main target is iOS and the ARM processor (32- and 64-bit), but there is also support for Mac OS X and Linux running on x86 CPUs (both 32- and 64-bit)

- Does not impose any restrictions on the Java platform features accessible to the developer, such as reflection or file I/O

- Supports standard JAR files that let the developer reuse the vast ecosystem of third-party Java libraries

- Provides access to the full native iOS APIs through a Java-to-Objective-C bridge, enabling the development of apps with truly native UIs and with full hardware access

- Integrates with the most popular tools such as NetBeans, Eclipse, Intellij IDEA, Maven, and Gradle

- App Store ready, with hundreds of apps already in the store

Limitations

Mainly due to the restrictions of the iOS platform, there are a few limitations when using RoboVM:

- Loading custom bytecode at runtime is not supported. All class files comprising the app have to be available at compile time on the developer machine.

- The Java Native Interface technology as used on the desktop or on servers usually loads native code from dynamic libraries, but Apple does not permit custom dynamic libraries to be shipped with an iOS app. RoboVM supports a variant of JNI based on static libraries.

- Another big limitation is that RoboVM is an alpha-state project under development and not yet recommended for production usage.

 RoboVM has full support for reflection.

How it works

As mentioned in *Chapter 4, Developing a JavaFX Application for Android*, since February 2015 there has been an agreement between the companies behind RoboVM and JavaFXPorts, and now a single plugin called jfxmobile-plugin allows us to build applications for three platforms—desktop, Android, and iOS—from the same codebase.

The JavaFXMobile plugin adds a number of tasks to your Java application that allow you to create .ipa packages that can be submitted to the Apple Store.

Android mostly uses Java as the main development language, so it is easy to merge your JavaFX 8 code with it. On iOS, the situation is internally totally different—but with similar Gradle commands.

The plugin will download and install the RoboVM compiler, and it will use RoboVM compiler commands to create an iOS application in `build/javafxports/ios`.

Getting started

In this section, you will learn how to install the RoboVM compiler using the `JavaFXMobile` plugin, and make sure the tool chain works correctly by reusing the same application, Phone Dial version 1.0, we developed previously for the Android platform in *Chapter 4, Developing a JavaFX Application for Android*.

Prerequisites

In order to use the RoboVM compiler to build iOS apps, the following tools are required:

- Oracle's Java SE JDK 8 update 45. Refer to *Chapter 1, Getting Started with JavaFX 8*, The *Installing Java SE 8 JDK* section.
- Gradle 2.4 or higher is required to build applications with the `jfxmobile` plugin. Refer to *Chapter 4, Developing a JavaFX Application for Android*, The Installing *Gradle 2.4* section.
- A Mac running **Mac OS X** 10.9 or later.
- **Xcode 6.x** from the Mac App Store (`https://itunes.apple.com/us/app/xcode/id497799835?mt=12`).

 The first time you install **Xcode**, and every time you update to a new version, you have to open it once to agree to the Xcode terms.

Preparing a project for iOS

We will reuse the project we developed before in *Chapter 4, Developing a JavaFX Application for Android*, for the Android platform, since there is no difference in code, project structure, or Gradle build script when targeting iOS.

They share the same properties and features, but with different Gradle commands that serve iOS development, and a minor change in the Gradle build script for the RoboVM compiler.

Therefore, we will see the power of **WORA** *Write Once, Run Everywhere* with the same application.

Project structure

Based on the same project structure from the Android example from *Chapter 4, Developing a JavaFX Application for Android*, the project structure for our iOS app should be as shown in the following figure:

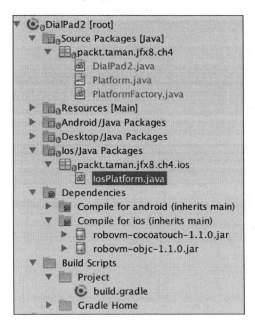

The application

We are going to reuse the same application from *Chapter 4, Developing a JavaFX Application for Android*: the Phone DialPad version 2.0 JavaFX 8 application:

As you can see, reusing the same codebase is a very powerful and useful feature, especially when you are developing to target many mobile platforms such as iOS and Android at the same time.

Interoperability with low-level iOS APIs

To have the same functionality of natively calling the default iOS phone dialer from our application as we did with Android, we have to provide the native solution for iOS as the following `IosPlatform` implementation:

```
import org.robovm.apple.foundation.NSURL;
import org.robovm.apple.uikit.UIApplication;
import packt.taman.jfx8.ch4.Platform;

public class IosPlatform implements Platform {

  @Override
  public void callNumber(String number) {
    if (!number.equals("")) {
      NSURL nsURL = new NSURL("telprompt://" + number);
```

```
        UIApplication.getSharedApplication().openURL(nsURL);
    }
  }
}
```

Gradle build files

We will use the same Gradle build script file that was used in *Chapter 4, Developing a JavaFX Application for Android*, but with a minor change by adding the following lines to the end of the script:

```
jfxmobile {
  ios {
    forceLinkClasses = [ 'packt.taman.jfx8.ch4.**.*' ]
  }
  android {
    manifest = 'lib/android/AndroidManifest.xml'
  }
}
```

All the work involved in installing and using robovm compilers is done by the jfxmobile plugin.

The purpose of those lines is to give the RoboVM compiler the location of the main application class that has to be loaded at runtime is, as it is not visible by default to the compiler.

The forceLinkClasses property ensures that those classes are linked in during RoboVM compilation.

Building the application

After we have added the necessary configuration set to build the script for iOS, its time to build the application in order to deploy it to different iOS target devices. To do so, we have to run the following command:

$ gradle build

We should have the following output:

```
BUILD SUCCESSFUL

Total time: 44.74 secs
```

We have built our application successfully; next, we need to generate the .ipa and, in the case of production, you have to test it by deploying it to as many iOS versions as you can.

Generating the iOS .ipa package file

In order to generate the final .ipa iOS package for our JavaFX 8 application, which is necessary for the final distribution to any device or the AppStore, you have to run the following `gradle` command:

```
gradle ios
```

This will generate the .ipa file in the directory `build/javafxports/ios`.

Deploying the application

During development, we need to check our application GUI and final application prototype on iOS simulators and measure the application performance and functionality on different devices. These procedures are very useful, especially for testers.

Let's see how it is a very easy task to run our application on either simulators or on real devices.

Deploying to a simulator

On a simulator, you can simply run the following command to check if your application is running:

```
$ gradle launchIPhoneSimulator
```

This command will package and launch the application in an *iPhone simulator* as shown in the following screenshot:

DialPad2 JavaFX 8 application running on the iOS 8.3/iPhone 4s simulator

This command will launch the application in an iPad simulator:

```
$ gradle launchIPadSimulator
```

Deploying to an Apple device

In order to package a JavaFX 8 application and deploy it to an Apple device, simply run the following command:

```
$ gradle launchIOSDevice
```

This command will launch the JavaFX 8 application in the device that is connected to your desktop/laptop.

Then, once the application is launched on your device, type in any number and then tap Call.

The iPhone will ask for permission to dial using the default mobile dialer; tap on **Ok**. The default mobile dialer will be launched and will the number as shown in the following figure:

Default mobile dialer

To be able to test and deploy your apps on your devices, you will need an active subscription with the Apple Developer Program. Visit the Apple Developer Portal, `https://developer.apple.com/register/index.action`, to sign up. You will also need to provision your device for development. You can find information on device provisioning in the Apple Developer Portal, or follow this guide: `http://www.bignerdranch.com/we-teach/how-to-prepare/ios-device-provisioning/`.

Summary

This chapter gave us a very good understanding of how JavaFX-based applications can be developed and customized using **RoboVM** for **iOS** to make it possible to run your applications on Apple platforms.

You learned about RoboVM features and limitations, and how it works; you also gained skills that you can use for developing.

You then learned how to install the required software and tools for iOS development and how to enable Xcode along with the *RoboVM* compiler, to package and install the Phone Dial JavaFX-8-based application on OS simulators.

We have seen how we reused the same application we already developed in *Chapter 4, Developing a JavaFX Application for Android*, proving that the Java WORA paradigm works.

Finally, we provided tips on how to run and deploy your application on real devices.

The next chapter will open a window on the IoT development world; we are going to see how to buy a RaspberryPi model 2, install and configure *raspbian-wheezy* OS for development, and how to install the Java SE for embedded devices. We will then develop a JavaFX 8 application that will run on our credit-card-sized microcomputer.

6
Running JavaFX Applications on the Raspberry Pi

Welcome to the **IoT (Internet of Things)** world. There is no doubt that you hear this term around all the time. IoT has become a hot topic of late, and for good reason too. Some estimates put the number of connected small devices somewhere around 9 billion currently; it's projected to jump to 24 billion devices by 2020. While the projections vary, the assessment really doesn't: in terms of sheer numbers, the IoT is going to dwarf any computing models ever seen.

Very closely related to the IoT world, we have the Raspberry Pi — a credit card-sized microcomputer designed by the Raspberry Pi Foundation for experimentation and education.

What you should know about the Raspberry Pi is that it is nothing but a small computer. Small power requirements, small physical size, small memory, and most importantly a low-cost device. Everything about it is small, but it is still just a computer and it uses Linux.

Java was made for IoT from the first day of its invention. Java was created with a clear vision in mind: to control small devices such as television set-top boxes. With the explosion of IoT, Java returns to its roots.

You may think that JavaFX, a platform for rich-client development, would miss the IoT party — but it is not so! According to the *JavaFX Overview* page on the Oracle Technology Network:

> *"It is designed to provide a lightweight, hardware-accelerated Java UI platform"*

This statement holds the key to graphically rich-and-powerful JavaFX: hardware acceleration and; luckily, the Raspberry Pi comes with a powerful GPU.

In this chapter, we will learn about:

- Buying, preparing, and configuring the Raspberry Pi
- Preparing the Raspberry Pi for JavaFX 8
- Connecting to the Raspberry Pi remotely
- Installing and configuring Java SE 8 on the Raspberry Pi
- Developing and running JavaFX 8 applications on the Raspberry Pi
- Using NetBeans with the Raspberry Pi

Excited? Need to have fun! Right, let's dive straight in and play with our Raspberry Pi.

 Since the release of JDK 8u33 for ARM version on January 2015, Oracle has removed JavaFX Embedded from the ARM distribution. See `http://www.oracle.com/technetwork/java/javase/jdk-8u33-arm-relnotes-2406696.html#CACHGFJC` and `http://jaxenter.com/jdk-arm-without-javafx-end-javafx-embedded-114212.html`.

Code for JavaFX Embedded has been given to the open source project OpenJFX (`https://wiki.openjdk.java.net/display/OpenJFX/Main`). It is recommended that developers who are looking for alternatives to JavaFX Embedded come out and contribute to the project.

In this chapter, we will learn a few ways to overcome this problem.

What is the Raspberry Pi?

As we mentioned previously, the Raspberry Pi is a computer a very small and low-cost computer. In fact, it is roughly the size of a credit card. Do not be fooled by its size; as we know, good things come in small packages. However, the Raspberry Pi does not come in a package at all.

It does not come in a case and its circuit board and chips are fully visible, as you can see in the following image. You can plug a Raspberry Pi into a digital TV or monitor and use a USB keyboard and mouse with it, making it very easy to use. Because of its small size, you can easily transport it anywhere.

The Raspberry Pi is a capable device that allows people of all ages to explore computing, and to learn how to program in languages such as Java, JavaFX, Python, and Scratch. In addition, it will do everything a desktop computer can do—from browsing the Internet and playing high-definition videos or games to working with spreadsheets or word processing software.

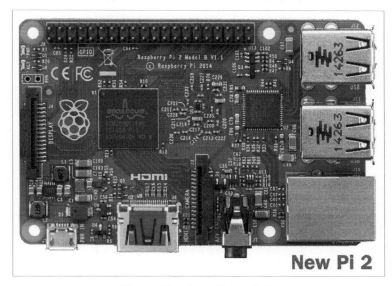

The new Raspberry Pi 2 model B

What can you do with it?

The Raspberry Pi gives you the opportunity to build and control a device that does what you want it to do. For example, you can deploy your very own robot arm, controlled by a program that you have written. You can design and create your own role-playing game, or produce beautiful computer art or music—all by using code.

Moreover, the Raspberry Pi Foundation's main aim is to make it fun for kids all over the world to learn to program and understand how computers work.

Why is the Raspberry Pi a perfect fit for JavaFX?

So what makes the Raspberry Pi such a perfect fit for Java and JavaFX? The answer can be found in the following points:

- It is faster than the specifications seem to indicate. As noted, the default clock speed for the Pi is 900 MHz. But with its 900 MHz clock speed that can be safely overclocked to 1 GHz and its 1 GB RAM, this small computer can run really bigger and powerful applications.

- Very wisely, the Foundation chose a CPU with floating-point support, often referred to as hard float, which offers greater performance than so-called soft float-only chips. Operating systems available for the Pi take advantage of that extra power and speed.

- Finally, the Pi has a fairly beefy Graphics Processing Unit (GPU) with a fast 3D core that is capable of BluRay quality playback, using H.264 at 40MBits/s (`http://www.Raspberry Pi.org/faqs#generalSoCUsed`).

Which module should you buy?

At the time of writing, there are five models of the Raspberry Pi: A, A+, B, B+, and since February 2015 the new model Pi 2 model B. Here is a comparison between the versions A+ and 2 B.

Model A+	Model 2 B
Costs ~$25	Costs ~$35
One USB port	Four USB ports
No Ethernet	Standard Ethernet connection
256 MB RAM	1 GB RAM

The model A+ is cheaper, but only has one USB port and no Ethernet connection. This may not be a problem. If you connect a powered USB hub to the Model A+ and then employ a USB-to-WiFi adapter, you have all the networking capabilities of Model B+. One main difference between the two models is the amount of RAM. Model A+ has 256 MB of RAM. The model B+ has a 512 MB RAM and 2 B has a 1 GB RAM. This is not upgradable on either model.

All Raspberry Pi microcomputers come with a slot for an SD memory card, audio out-jack, video ports for RCA and HDMI, and a row of pins for general purpose input and output. There are two additional connectors for display and a camera, but both require highly specialized hardware. Given a small price difference, typically $10 to $25, I recommend getting the model 2 B to start with. If you are purchasing more than one for, say, a classroom, the model A+ may be sufficient.

You can buy a kit with all you need to start from any online store for no more than $100, and it would include:

- The new Raspberry Pi 2 (RPi2) quad-core 900 MHz 1GB RAM and CanaKit WiFi adapter

- Premium-quality 6-foot HDMI cable, GPIO to breadboard interface board, ribbon cable, breadboard, jumper wires, GPIO Quick Reference Card, and Resistor Colors Quick Reference Card

- 8 GB Samsung MicroSD card (a Raspberry Pi Foundation-recommended MicroSD card preloaded with NOOBS), a high-quality Raspberry Pi 2 case, and heat sink

- RGB LED, 8 LEDs (blue/red/yellow/green), 15 resistors, 2 push button switches, and General Guide for Beginners to Electronic Components

- 2.5A USB power supply with 5-foot micro USB cable specially designed for the Raspberry Pi 2 (UL listed)

Typical kit components for a Raspberry Pi B Model 2

Buying the Raspberry Pi

The Raspberry Pi Foundation in the United Kingdom makes the Raspberry Pi. Unfortunately, it has a history of being back-ordered. Fortunately, you can buy from several vendors and a few of them are listed on the main page of rasberrypi.org. You can also buy it from `http://www.amazon.com`, although you will have to pay a bit more. Prices vary from what you will see here.

Finally, check out `http://www.adafruit.com`. They are reasonably priced and also carry some useful accessories that you will need in your future projects. In these stores you can also find starter kits including the Raspberry Pi and the necessary components to start.

Related websites and documentation

The Internet contains a wealth of information about the Raspberry Pi. As you work on more advanced topics, you will find it helpful to know where to find answers.

The official website for the Raspberry Pi Foundation is `http://www.rasberrypi.org`. It lists sources from which to purchase the Raspberry Pi microcomputer. It has a variety of tutorials and helpful forums.

For more information about the version of Linux running on the Raspberry Pi, visit `http://elinux.org/index.php?title=RPi_Hub&redirect=no`. There is information about the general-purpose and input/output pins; Raspbian Wheezy, the version of Linux designed for the Raspberry Pi; and sample projects. You will also find information about other embedded systems, such as the **Minnow board** and **BeagleBoard**.

Neil Black has created a stellar beginner's guide to the Raspberry Pi and deserves a round of applause. Please visit `http://neil-black.co.uk/the-updated-raspberry-pi-beginners-guide` if you ever find yourself confused during the setup process.

Finally, visit `http://www.adafruit.com` to buy the Raspberry Pi as well as power supplies, motor control boards, and experimentation kits. If you cannot buy parts locally, this group is an excellent place to purchase accessories and other components.

Preparing the Raspberry Pi for JavaFX 8

Your Raspberry Pi will do nothing without an operating system, which is loaded from the SD Card. We need a way to interact with it by first installing the supported operating system, which in our case is Raspbian Wheezy; all official supported operating systems for the Pi are listed and can be downloaded from the link `http://www.raspberrypi.org/downloads/`.

Then, we will configure the network settings for our Pi to connect it remotely. Finally, we will check the Java SE 8 version installed by default and proceed to check for updates, if not prepackaged with OS already.

As mentioned before, the last update doesn't include JavaFX so we will find a way to add it. Let's start preparing our SD card to install the Raspbian Wheezy operating system and have the Raspberry Pi up and running.

Creating a bootable SD card

Now, we are going to prepare our SD card with the Raspbian Wheezy OS, which will allow us to interact with our Raspberry Pi. This is a very important step. There are two ways to do this:

Using NOOBS

NOOBS is an easy operating system installer that contains Raspbian. But the lite version doesn't bundle a Raspbian. It also provides a selection of alternative operating systems, which are then downloaded from the Internet and installed.

Beginners should start with the NOOBS method, but it requires an Internet connection with good speed to download the preferred OS.

If you have bought a kit that comes with a preinstalled NOOBS SD card, you can skip to the next step. Alternatively, if you need an SD card, you can order one from the Swag store at `http://swag.raspberrypi.org/products/noobs-8gb-sd-card` or even download and set it up to your SD card yourself. All steps are provided at the link `http://www.raspberrypi.org/help/noobs-setup/`.

Burning Raspbian Wheezy OS to your SD card:

This is my favorite setup as I have already downloaded the OS and will burn it directly to my SD card; here are the steps to do it from Mac OS X (make sure you have a valid SD card, with 4/8/16 GB memory and of class 10):

We need to have our SD card formatted in FAT32. We will do this easily with SD Formatter 4.0 for either Windows or Mac, which is available for download from the SD Association's site at `https://www.sdcard.org/downloads/formatter_4/eula_mac/index.html`.

Follow the instructions to install the software package:

1. Insert your SD card into the computer or laptop's SD card reader and *make a note of the drive letter* allocated to it—for example, `/disk2` in my case.

2. In **SDFormatter**, select the drive letter for your SD card, go to **Format Option** and select **Overwrite format**, name it `RaspWheezy` (optional), and click on **Format**. It may take a while to format the SD depending on the size of the card.

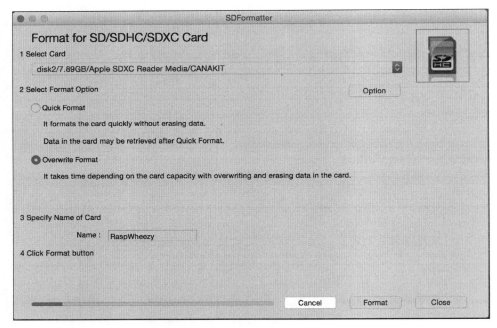

Formatting SD card with SDFormatter application

3. Once the format is completed, close SDFormatter. If you are on Mac or Linux, run the following command line from your terminal to check the disk letter and format type:

```
$ diskutil list
```

In this case, the SD card is `/dev/disk2`, with the `DOS_FAT_32` format type and `RASPWHEEZY` as the name. On Windows. Open Windows Explorer and check the drive.

> Do not get this wrong, or you may destroy all the data on the wrong `disk/card/drive`.

4. Download Raspbian Wheezy OS from the link `http://downloads.raspberrypi.org/raspbian_latest`, unzip it, and you should have the `2015-02-16-raspbian-wheezy.img` file.

5. From the command line on Mac or Linux, unmount the disk but don't eject:

    ```
    $ diskutil unmountDisk /dev/disk2
    ```

6. Then write the image to the SD card with the `dd` command line:

    ```
    $ sudo dd if=/path/to/2015-02-16-raspbian-wheezy.img of=/dev/rdisk2 bs=1m
    ```

    Once you have typed your password, the writing process begins and you have to wait till you get the prompt again. As this will take a few minutes, on Windows, you can use Win32DiskImager (It can be downloaded from `http://www.raspberry-projects.com/pi/pi-operating-systems/win32diskimager`).

7. After the `dd` command finishes, eject the card:

    ```
    $ sudo diskutil eject /dev/rdisk2
    ```

> Note that `dd` will not feedback any information until there is an error or it is finished; information will be shown and the disk will remount when complete. However, if you wish to view the progress, you can use the *Ctrl + T* shortcut. This generates **SIGINFO**, the status argument of your `tty`, and will display information about the process.

Congratulations, now mount your SD card to the Raspberry Pi and connect it to a proper monitor to start it up.

Configuring the Raspberry Pi

Now, we need to set up the Pi for the first booting time and also configure a static IP in order to connect to it from our laptop and remotely:

1. Mount the SD card we prepared previously.
2. Plug in your keyboard, mouse, and monitor cables.

3. Plug your WiFi Adapter into one of the USB ports.

4. Now, plug in the power cable to your Pi.

5. You should see some verbose output on the screen booting up the Raspbian OS. Proceed boldly and with no fear.

6. On the first boot, the Raspberry Pi configuration screen will show up and will gave you a series of options that you can use to configure your Raspberry Pi. Basically, you will want to set up your time-zone and own locale configuration. Review the settings of memory split between CPU and GPU, or enable SSH. But for the most part, you can simply ignore them, move to the last step with the arrow keys, and hit Return.

7. If you selected something you don't like during the configuration process, you can restart the configuration by typing from the console `sudo raspi-config`.

8. If the Raspberry Pi was correctly configured, you'll see a series of Linux boot messages scroll by followed by a request to log in. The default user log in is `pi` and the password is `raspberry`. Now, you'll be presented with a standard Linux prop. Congratulations, your Raspberry Pi is up-and-running.

9. Wheezy comes with a graphical user interface. Simply type `sudo startx` and you'll see a colorful user interface complete with games, word processors, and web browsers, as shown in the following screenshot:

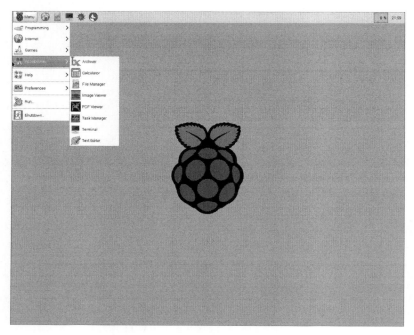

Raspberry Pi Desktop

The Raspberry Pi Desktop is the **Lightweight X11 Desktop Environment (LXDE)**. Spend some time exploring it. You'll find it very familiar, although a bit slower than your high-powered desktop computer.

When you're done with LXDE, simply log out and you'll be back at the Linux prompt. For the sake of the information on your SD card, it's important to gracefully shut down your Raspberry Pi. Before you yank out the power cord, issue a shutdown command:

```
$ Sudo shutdown -h now.
```

This will make sure that everything is written to the SD card before all the processes are shut down. Now, you can safely pull out the power cord and that's the extent of the on/off switch for the Raspberry Pi.

Congratulations, you have finished your first session with your Raspberry Pi.

Connecting to the Raspberry Pi remotely

Usually, you will connect to your Raspberry Pi using peripherals and monitor, but this will not always be the case since you will need to control your Pi from your computer, browser, or even mobile at the development stage or when the Pi itself is used as a cool server controlling your home appliances.

Giving your Raspberry Pi a fixed network address isn't necessary, but it is strongly recommended. Doing so means you always connect to your Pi using the same address (or name, if you create an entry in your hosts file), and thus it removes one potential variable from your development process.

It's also a good idea to update your network DHCP device/router with the Pi's IP address so that it doesn't try to assign it to another device on your network. The steps required to do so will vary by switch/router manufacturer.

We will install VNC server on our Raspberry Pi. **Virtual Network Computing (VNC)** allows you to control one computer from another over a network. It provides a graphical user interface, including the mouse and keyboard. In our case, it will allow us to see and use the Raspberry Pi GUI without the need for a physical keyboard and mouse connected to the Raspberry Pi.

Right now, this is a convenience and if you're happy with your current mouse, keyboard, and monitor setup, you can skip this part. When you begin experimenting with devices that require one or more USB ports, VNC will become a necessity.

There are five steps to set up VNC:

1. Connect to a home WiFi Internet connection.
2. Install VNC on the Raspberry Pi.
3. Set up to start at boot.
4. Set up a static IP address.
5. Connect to VNC with a client.

Connecting to WiFi Internet connection, Raspbian Wheezy includes a WiFi configuration utility. Also, all Raspbians released after October 28, 2012 are prebundled with this utility.

 Setting up WiFi requires that your router is broadcasting the SSID. Make sure you have *Broadcast SSID* set up on your router! This will not work with private SSID setups.

Now, Let's connect to the Raspberry Pi remotely:

1. From the Raspbian desktop, go to **Menu | Preferences | WiFi Configuration**, as shown in the following screenshot:

Choosing the WiFi Configuration utility

2. Double-click on the icon and you will see the following window:

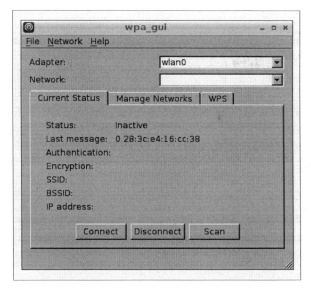

WiFi Configuration utility GUI

3. Click on the **Scan** button and a second window will open. Find your wireless access point in the list and double-click on it. This will open another window:

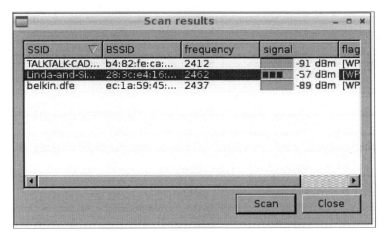

List of access points

4. Enter your password in the PSK field and then click on **Add**. When you look at the first window, you should see that the connection is all set up for use.

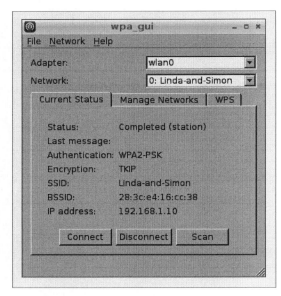

Final status in adding an access point

You can connect or disconnect using the buttons. You can see in the preceding screenshot that the IP address of the Pi is shown at the bottom of the window.

Note that there's a manual procedure to set up the WiFi connection on a terminal. This requires editing the config files and manually adding the SSID and password of the network. For more information, go to https://www.raspberrypi.org/documentation/configuration/wireless/wireless-cli.md.

Congratulations, your Pi is connected to Internet. Now let's install a VNC server.

Installing VNC on the Raspberry Pi

Now that you have an Internet connection, you can install a VNC server on your Raspberry Pi. If you're using Raspbian Wheezy, this is simple. At a command prompt, enter the following line:

```
$ sudo apt-get install tightvncserver
```

You'll get the message: **Do you want to continue? Yes or No?**

Let's answer with a capital *Y* and take a break. When the installation is complete, enter the following command:

```
$ vncserver
```

You'll be asked to create a password, I use *raspberry*. It notes that the password is longer than eight characters; go ahead and retype `raspberry`. Next, you'll be asked: **Would you like to enter a view only password?** Enter *N* for no.

Congratulations, you're running VNC on your Raspberry Pi.

Setting up VNC to start at boot

As you become more advanced, you may not always need VNC but let's assume you want VNC to run every time you start your Raspberry Pi:

1. Edit the `rc.local` file using the following command from the Pi **LX Terminal**:

    ```
    $ sudo nano /etc/rc.local
    ```

2. Scroll to the bottom and add the following line above `exit 0`:

    ```
    su -c "/usr/bin/tightvncserver -geometry 1280x1024" pi
    ```

3. Save the file and restart your Raspberry Pi using the following command:

    ```
    $ sudo shutdown -r now
    ```

4. Now, every time you start your Raspberry Pi, VNC will be available.

Setting up a static IP address

Connecting with the Raspberry Pi over VNC requires a static IP address, one that doesn't change. I'll show you how to get that for wired and wireless networking in the next few steps:

1. If you are on a home network, you'll need to discover a usable IP address. To do this, turn to your Raspberry Pi, open Pi LX Terminal, and type:

    ```
    mohamed_taman$ ifconfig -a
    ```

    Then, type the following command:

    ```
    mohamed_taman$ netstat -nr
    ```

2. Gather the following information: *current IP* (if you want to keep it), *netmask*, *gateway*, *destination*, and *broadcast*. Write these down, you'll need them soon!

3. On the Pi, make a backup of `/etc/network/interfaces` by running the following command:

   ```
   $ sudo cp /etc/network/interfaces /etc/network/interfaces.org
   ```

4. Modify the `interfaces` file with the following command:

   ```
   $ sudo nano /etc/network/interfaces
   ```

5. Change the `interfaces` file from:

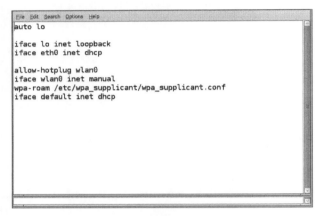

Interfaces file before editing

6. Select the IP numbers that suit your network; also change `wpa-ssid` to your wireless network name and `wpa-psk` to wireless password:

Interfaces file after editing

7. Save the file and restart your Raspberry Pi. These settings work for both wired and wireless connections. Congratulations, you can now connect to your Pi with the VNC client.

Auto login in the Raspberry Pi

Like most people, you might have bought the Raspberry Pi to build your own appliance for home or office. The next thing you should do is set up the Raspberry Pi, connect your peripherals, and install or develop the necessary software.

What you want at the end of your project is to power on the appliance and have it should show you all the magic you were expecting.

The spoiler comes when the Pi boots to the login prompt and waits for you to enter the username and password. So, let's automate the Raspberry Pi login:

1. From your Pi, open a terminal and edit the `inittab` file with the following command:

   ```
   sudo nano /etc/inittab
   ```

2. Disable the `getty` program by navigating to the following line in `inittab`:

   ```
   1:2345:respawn:/sbin/getty 115200 tty1
   ```

3. Add a # at the beginning of the line to comment it out, as shown in the following line:

   ```
   #1:2345:respawn:/sbin/getty 115200 tty1
   ```

4. Add a login program to `inittab` just below the commented line:

   ```
   1:2345:respawn:/bin/login -f pi tty1 </dev/tty1 >/dev/tty1 2>&1
   ```

5. This will run the login program with `pi` user and without any authentication.

6. Save and exit by pressing *Ctrl* + *X*, followed by *Y* to save the file, and then press *Enter* to confirm the filename.

Reboot the Pi and it will boot straight to the shell prompt `pi@raspberrypi` without prompting you to enter your username or password.

Connecting to VNC with a client

Before going any further, let's make sure everything is working correctly. To do this, you'll need a VNC client. If you're using a Macintosh with a recent version of Mac OS X, this is simple.

Go to **Finder** | **Go** | **Connect to Server**. Enter `vnc://` and the IP address you have given to your Raspberry Pi. In my case, it was 192.168.2.150 followed by a colon and the number 5901, as shown in the following screenshot. The full URL should be **vnc://192.168.2.150:5901**.

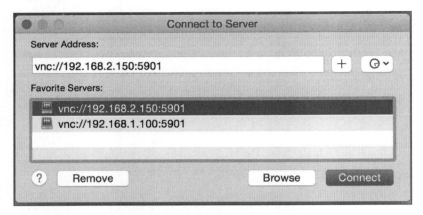

Connect to the Pi VNC server.

As shown in the image `5901` is the number of the port the Raspberry Pi VNC server is listening to. Hit **Connect**. Don't worry about the screen sharing encryption, hit **Connect** again. Now type in the password you created earlier (`raspberry`). If everything is working correctly, you'll see a large raspberry. Congratulations!

If you're not on a Macintosh computer, you'll need to download a VNC client. You can obtain free viewers from `http://realvnc.com/`. There are clients for Windows, iOS, Android, and the Chrome browser. Yes, you can control your Raspberry Pi from your cell phone.

JavaFX 8 development prerequisites

Now as we have set up and configured our Raspberry Pi for development, we need to install the same correct matching JDK 8 build version on both our development machine and the Pi. This is very important to avoid library/versioning issues when running our JavaFX 8 application, and this is what we are going to do next.

Installing Java SE 8 on the Raspberry Pi

At the time of writing, Raspbian Wheezy is shipped with JDK 8 preinstalled. To check, simply type the following at your Pi command prompt:

```
pi@raspberrypi ~ $ java -version
```

You will see something like this, depending upon the version that is currently installed and accessible:

Raspbian Wheezy Java version on Raspberry Pi

The important bit is the second line: if it doesn't say 1.8.n, you'll need to install JDK8.

Installing Java SE 8

We have already installed our JDK 8 before and all necessary steps are described in the *Installing Java SE 8 JDK* section in *Chapter 1, Getting Started with JavaFX 8*.

Adding JavaFX

As mentioned previously, Oracle has withdrawn its support for JavaFX Embedded. If you have installed JDK 8u45 or the prebundled version installed on Raspbian Wheezy, there is no `jfxrt.jar` bundled, so we need to provide it in order to run JavaFX applications on our Pi.

One-way to do this is to follow the tutorial at `https://wiki.openjdk.java.net/display/OpenJFX/Cross+Building+for+ARM+Hard+Float`), cross-building OpenJFX for ARM. This is for really advanced developers.

An easier way is to download a prebuilt distribution such as `armv6hf-sdk.zip` hosted on the JavaFXPorts project (`https://bitbucket.org/javafxports/arm/downloads`).

Once you have downloaded `armv6hf-sdk.zip`, unzip it and add this command-line option to attach the external source to the `classpath` with the extension mechanism:

```
-Djava.ext.dirs=<path to armv6hf-sdk>/rt/lib/ext
```

Alternatively, you can copy the contents of `rt/lib/ext` and `rt/lib/arm` from this zip into your JVM folders, avoiding the use of the extension mechanism.

Configuring NetBeans for the Raspberry Pi

NetBeans 8 adds the capability to point to a remote JDK and use it to debug and execute programs remotely that you write locally on your development machine. It even deploys your applications automatically and seamlessly. As documented by José Pereda in his article at `http://netbeans.dzone.com/articles/nb-8-raspberry-pi-end2end`, you can enable this capability with the following steps:

1. Start NetBeans on your machine.

2. Choose **Tools** from the menu bar and then select **Java Platforms**. Click on the **Add Platform** button.

3. Select the **Remote Java Standard Edition** radio button and click on **Next**.

4. Provide the following entries (shown in the following screenshot as an example):

    Platform Name: JavaFX on Raspberry Pi JDK 8

    Host: Enter the static IP address or hostname of your Raspberry Pi you already assigned before

    Username: pi

    Password: raspberry

    Remote JRE Path: /usr/lib/jvm/jdk-8-oracle-arm-vfp-hflt/jre

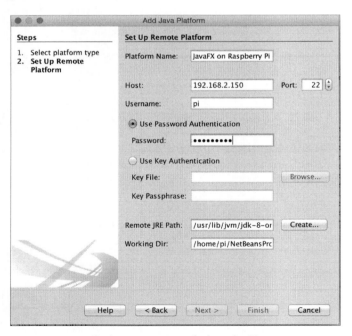

Setting up a remote platform for Pi

5. Click on the **Finish** button and wait for NetBeans to establish and configure the remote JDK connection.

6. Click on the **Close** button once the remote JDK is in place.

Now that we've completed the setup, you should have a development environment that is among the best available to develop JavaFX 8 applications for the Raspberry Pi. So let's get started!

The switch application

The switch application is very simple in its nature, but the idea is mainly divided into two main points: how to run JavaFX 8 applications on Raspberry Pi and how to control the outside world from the Raspberry Pi **General-purpose input/output (GPIO)**. We will use a project called **Pi4j** for such purpose.

The idea is simple; we are going to create a JavaFX application that will act as a switch controller to control a LED associated to an electrical circuit connected to your Raspberry Pi.

The following screenshots show the application in the ON and OFF states:

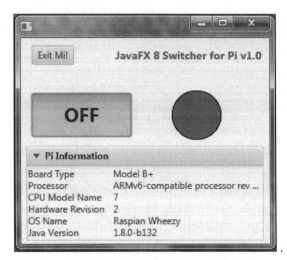

Switch Application ON state

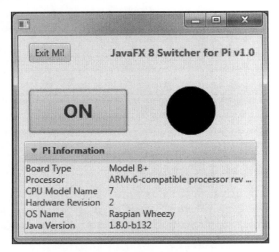

Switch Application OFF state

What is the Pi4J library?

The Pi4j library (`http://pi4j.com`) is a project intended to provide a bridge between the native libraries and Java for full access to the Raspberry Pi features and controls, so you can easily access the GPIO pins for your Java project.

Visit `http://pi4j.com/pins/model-2b-rev1.html` for Raspberry Pi 2 model B (J8 header) for GPIO pin numbering. Also, your kit's GPIO adapter may come with a GPIO header quick reference.

For this example, you will need some basic electronic components such as a LED, a resistor, and a breadboard. If those are not included in your kit, you can acquire them from online stores.

Circuit setup

Now we need to set up our circuit by adding a LED with a 220 Ohms pull-up resistor in a breadboard, and connect the anode to GPIO pin #1 and cathode to the GPIO GND pin, as shown in the following figure (CanaKit comes with a general assembly guide for the most commonly used electronic parts):

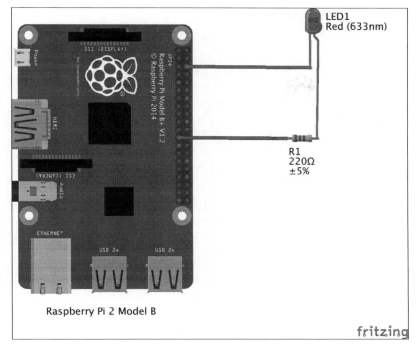

Switcher application circuit setup

The application

As previously mentioned, the application UI contains two buttons. **Exit Me!** is responsible for shutting down the GPIO controller and closing the application. The second button is a toggle button (**ON/OFF**) that works as a switch. It has two states: when selected, its state is true and it becomes false when not selected. Additionally, we change its label programmatically to indicate the state of the current controlled LED.

In addition, there is one circle shape that mimics the physical LED state. So, when the toggle button is ON, then the circle will be filled with red. OFF turns it to black, which is the default state.

Finally, at the bottom of the application scene, we add a TitledPane labeled Pi Information displaying some Raspberry Pi information.

By looking at the `SwitchUIController.java` class, you will find that we have very important fields to declare before interacting with the `Pi4J` library:

```
private GpioController gpio;
private GpioPinDigitalOutput pin;
```

The first line is responsible for creating a new GPIO controller instance, which is done in the `initialize()` method via `GpioFactory` as it includes a `createInstance` method to create the GPIO controller:

```
gpio = GpioFactory.getInstance();
```

 Your project should only instantiate a single GPIO controller instance and that instance should be shared across your project.

To access a GPIO pin, you must first provision the pin. Provisioning configures the pin based on how you intend to use it. Provisioning can automatically export the pin, set its direction, and set up any edge detection for interrupt-based events:

```
// provision gpio pin #01 as an output pin and turn on
pin = gpio.provisionDigitalOutputPin(GPIO_01);
```

This is how to provision an output pin #1. Your program will be able to control the state only of those pins that are provisioned as output pins. Output pins are used for controlling relays, LEDs, and transistors.

Now all we want to do is to control the LED from our application using the toggle button. This is done via the `doOnOff()` event function that is registered to toggle the button, as shown in the following code:

```
@FXML
private void doOnOff(ActionEvent event) {
    if (switchTgl.isSelected()) {
        pin.high();
        led.setFill(RED);
        switchTgl.setText("OFF");
        System.out.println("Switch is On");
    } else {
        pin.low();
        led.setFill(BLACK);
        switchTgl.setText("ON");
        System.out.println("Switch is Off");
    }
}
```

The P14J library provides a number of convenience methods for controlling or writing a state to a GPIO pin. In our application, we use `pin.high()` to turn the LED on and `pin.low()` to turn the LED off.

Finally, when the application exits, we have to shut down the GPIO controller. The Pi4J project provides an implementation to automatically set GPIO pin states as inactive when the application is terminated.

This is useful to ensure that the GPIO pins states are not active or leaving some activity engaged if the program is shutdown. We can simply do this with the following line of code from the GPIO instance we have created previously:

```
gpio.shutdown();
```

When you press the toggle button to turn ON the LED, you will see your green LED glows. When it is OFF, you will see that the LED is faded.

Application circuit—LED OFF

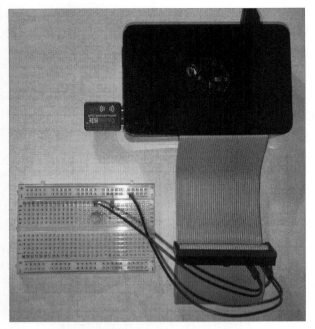

Application circuit—LED ON

Next, let's configure our project to run our JavaFX switch application directly on the Raspberry Pi from NetBeans.

Using NetBeans with the Pi

After discussing our application logic and seeing how it works, it's time for the best part: building your application and running it on the Raspberry Pi using NetBeans. The steps are as follows:

1. Right-click on the Chapter6 project in NetBeans **Projects** tab and select **Properties**.

2. From the **Project Properties** box, select **Run** from the **Categories** menu to the left. You will see a dialog similar to the following screenshot:

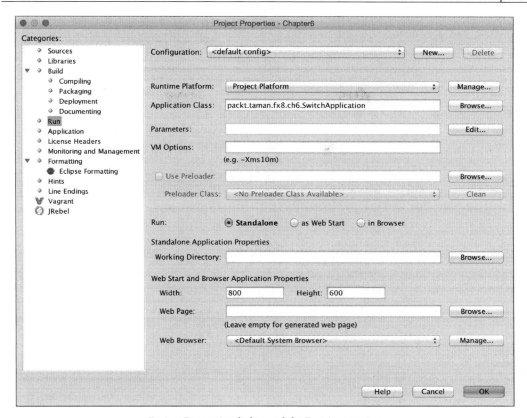

Project Properties dialog and the Run incarnation

3. Click on the **New** button to the right of the selected **Configuration**. Set a
   name for the **New Configuration** (Pi Remote Config) and click on the **OK**
   button, as shown in the following screenshot:

New Configuration

4. Now you have to associate a remote JDK with your remote configuration. To do so, click on the combo box labeled **Runtime Platform** and select `JavaFX on Raspberry Pi JDK 8` that you configured earlier. Don't forget to add the path for `jfxrt.jar` in **VM Options**:

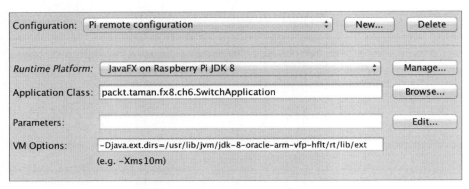

Remote Pi JDK association

5. The final step is to build and deploy the application to the Raspberry Pi. To do so, go to the **Run** menu, select **Run Project,** and watch the NetBeans Output window/tab. If you keep an eye on the Pi's screen when running the application, you will see the following output messages:

```
jfx-deployment-script:
jfx-deployment:
jar:
Connecting to 192.168.2.150:22
cmd : mkdir -p '/home/pi/NetBeansProjects/Chapter6/dist'
Connecting to 192.168.2.150:22
done.
profile-rp-calibrate-passwd:
Connecting to 192.168.2.150:22
cmd : cd '/home/pi/NetBeansProjects/Chapter6';
'/usr/lib/jvm/jdk-8-oracle-arm-vfp-hflt/jre/bin/
java'  -Dfile.encoding=UTF-8 -jar /home/pi/
NetBeansProjects/Chapter6/dist/Chapter6.jar
```

Summary

In this chapter, we took a credit card-sized microcomputer no larger than a deck of playing cards and transformed it into a JavaFX Switch controller machine. Along the way, you learned about the Raspberry Pi, how to create a bootable SD card, how to install an operating system to it, how to configure it for best performance and remote connectivity, how to give it a fixed network (IP) address, and how to connect to the Pi from your development machine.

We also revisited how to install JDK 8/ JavaFX 8 to both the Raspberry Pi and your development machine, and you learned how to install and configure NetBeans on your development machine so that it can use the JDK on the Pi as a remote platform for debugging and execution.

With both your development machine and the Raspberry Pi ready for action, we discussed the principles needed to develop a simple but great application to control the outside world from the Raspberry Pi using JavaFX and a few select tools/APIs, including Pi4j, to control GPIO.

Finally, you saw how to remotely deploy your application from NetBeans to your Raspberry Pi, all with just a few clicks.

In the next chapter, we are going to monitor a temperature sensor, measuring how hot your blood is from an Arduino board.

7
Monitoring and Controlling Arduino with JavaFX

Arduino is an open source electronics tool based on a simple programmable microcontroller board that can be programmed using a free open source IDE. Alone or attached to a computer, it creates interactive devices that can sense by taking inputs from a variety of switches or sensors and can act by controlling a variety of lights, motors, and other outputs physical devices.

As one of the first **Internet of Things (IoT)** devices, it was created in 2005. It has been here from the very beginning of the IoT concept.

Arduino runs standalone or can communicate with software running on your computer (Java, JavaFX, Python, and so on) and the boards can be assembled by hand or purchased preassembled.

It is a fact that Arduino simplifies the process of working with microcontrollers. Also, it more lucrative than other systems for teachers, students, and interested amateurs, as it is *inexpensive* — an Arduino board cost less than $50.

A simple, clear, and easy-to-use programming environment; an open source and extensible software; and open source and extensible hardware these features, among others, make Arduino support the do-it-yourself and do-it-with-others concepts that define the maker movement.

This chapter will show you how to develop a desktop application using JavaFX along with an Arduino board in order to monitor data coming from a real world temperature sensor and report it on a chart, *How HOT blooded you really are!*

In this chapter, you will:

- Get familiar with Arduino boards and their components
- Install and prepare the Arduino software and environment, IDE, and drivers
- Develop an Arduino blood meter sketch to control and monitor the circuit
- Read Arduino data into a JavaFX application using serial communication
- Present data using the JavaFX Charting API

What is an Arduino board?

The Arduino Uno, the most well-known Arduino board, is a microcontroller board based on the **ATmega328** datasheet (`http://www.atmel.com/dyn/resources/prod_documents/doc8161.pdf`), which is the brains of the board. It is about 3 x 2 inches in size. It has 14 digital input/output pins, 6 analog input pins, and 32 kilobytes of flash memory.

Each board contains a reset button. In addition, it includes a USB port so that, when it is connected to a computer, it becomes a source of power as well as a communication tool. If you are not connected to a computer, you can use an alternate power source such as an AC 9-to-12 V DC adapters that can be connected by plugging a 2.1 mm center-positive plug into the board's power jack, or a 9 V battery pack.

The six digital pins with tilde symbol next to the number are the pins that allow for **Pulse Width Modulation (PWM)**, which is a technique for controlling power and simulating an analog signal on a digital input pin. One reason for using these pins might be to control the brightness of LED's.

The official specs for the Arduino Uno can be found on the `http://arduino.cc` website at `http://arduino.cc/en/Main/ArduinoBoardUno`. Visit `http://www.arduino.cc/en/Main/Products` to find information about other Arduino boards, such as **Mega**, **Due**, or **Yun**, as well as the next releases **Tre** and **Zero**.

The following images show the Arduino Uno R3 board:

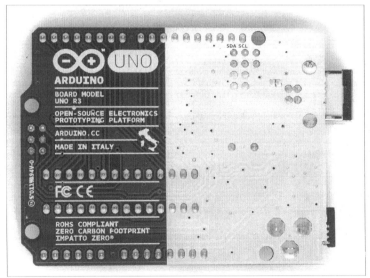

What can you do with it?

Your Arduino board might be small, but don't let its size deceive you. It is powerful and has a lot of room for growth. It is especially powerful because it is built on an open hardware and open software platform. We won't be spending time talking about open source; in a nutshell, it means that the information about the hardware and software is freely available and easy to find.

Arduino can be used to sense the environment by receiving input. It can also control output such as lights, motors, sensors, and more.

You can program the microcontroller on the board using the open source Arduino programming language.

Related websites and documentation

One of the great advantages of an open source and open hardware platform is that you can find information on the Internet.

A great place to start looking for information about Arduino is the official page: `http://arduino.cc` website at `http://arduino.cc/en/Guide/HomePage`. As your skills grow, you will want to work on more advanced topics and you'll find it helpful to know where to find answers.

Another great site is `http://adafruit.com`. This site has tutorials, examples, helpful forums, and a store to buy the parts you need.

Another interesting and fun application for kids is to combine **Lego Mindstorm** sensors and motors to the Arduino. I recommend the site `http://wayneandlayne.com`, as it has been the inspiration and starting point for my integration of Lego and Arduino. If you are looking for parts and projects, this is a great site to visit.

Setting up your Arduino

If this is your first exposure to Arduino, I strongly suggest that you start with a kit rather than assembling all the individual components.

Most of the activities in this chapter can be completed with a kit called the Arduino Starter Kit from arduino.cc, as shown in the following image. It includes an Arduino Uno R3 and other components to accomplish most of the prebundled projects. For a full description of the kit, visit `http://store.arduino.cc/product/K000007`.

Arduino Starter kit (Kit including components, Board, and projects book)

Buying an Arduino

While an Arduino Uno costs around $25, you can purchase different kits, including the board—starting from a basic Budget Pack ($50) to the Starter Pack for Arduino ($65) from `http://adafruit.com` or a Starter Kit ($90) from `http://arduino.cc`. These kits have the same components as the budget pack. But they also include some extras for more advanced tinkering.

One nice advantage of the starter kit from `http://arduino.cc` is that it includes a guidebook that features 15 different projects of varying skill levels.

If you are an Amazon user, you can usually find the same kits available on their site, but the prices may vary.

Most of the boards have core components in the same locations. So, more advanced boards have lengthened in size to accommodate additional components.

Here are some sites for purchasing components and some books: `http://arduino.cc`, `http://Adafruit.com`, `http://makershed.com`, `http://sparkfun.com`, and `http://Amazon.com`.

Other components you will need

In addition to the Arduino, you will also need a computer with Windows, Mac OS, or Linux, with the USB port to connect your computer to the board.

For the blood meter project, you will need some of the components that already come in the Arduino Starter kit. Here is a short list of the components you should have handy.

A computer with a USB port, a USB cable, a solderless breadboard, flexible wires, a TMP36 temperature sensor, three 220 Ohms resistors, and three LEDs (yellow, blue, and red), as shown in the following image:

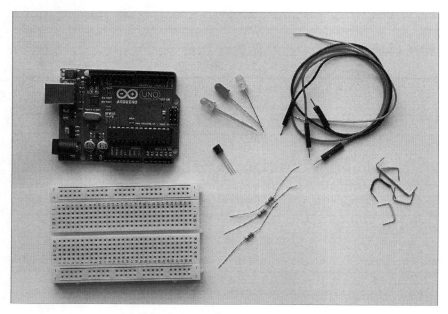

The blood meter project tools and material

The Arduino IDE

In order to interact and program the Arduino microcontroller, we need to download and install the Arduino Integrated Development Environment.

The Arduino software includes all the components you need to write code, a text editor, and compiler to convert it to machine language, and upload it to your board and run the code.

Downloading the IDE

At the time writing, the Arduino IDE version is 1.6.3 but you can get the latest version of the Arduino software from the link `http://www.arduino.cc/en/Main/Software`. Besides the Arduino version shown in the following screenshot, click on the preferred operating system link; in my case, I have chosen Mac OS X.

From the donation page, either donate or just click on the **JUST DOWNLOAD** link to start downloading the IDE; in my case, I chose `arduino-1.6.4-macosx.zip`.

After downloading, unzip the file and copy the `Arduino.app` file to the application folder on your Mac or link the Arduino executable to a location easy for you to access.

Once you have the IDE downloaded, you still need to take care of a few more hardware issues before you can start programming.

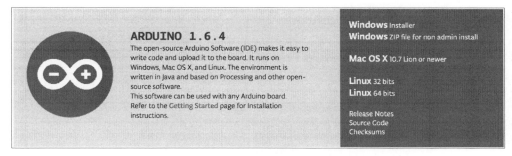

Download the Arduino IDE 1.6.4

Installing the drivers

First you need to connect the Arduino board to your computer using the USB cable. The green LED power indicator (labeled PWR or ON) should be on.

Windows Setup

Let's set up the Arduino in Windows:

1. Plug in your board and wait for Windows to begin its driver installation process.

2. Click on the **Start Menu** and open up the **Control Panel**.

3. From the **Control Panel**, navigate to **System and Security**. Next, click on **System**. Once the System window is open, select **Device Manager**.

4. Look under **Ports (COM & LPT)**. You should see an open port named `Arduino UNO (COMxx)`. If there is no **COM & LPT** section, look under **Other Devices** for **Unknown Device**.

5. Right-click on the **Arduino UNO (COMxx)** port and choose the **Update Driver Software** option.

6. Next choose the **Browse my computer for Driver software** option.

7. Finally, navigate to and select the driver file named `arduino.inf`, which is located in the `Drivers` folder of the Arduino software download (not the `FTDI USB Drivers` sub-directory).

8. Windows will finish the driver installation from there.

 If you have Windows 8 and the driver is not well installed, try to disable the driver signature enforcement.

Mac OS X and Linux setup

For both the Mac OS X and Linux operating systems, no drivers have to be installed.

For Mac OS X, when you connect the Arduino board, you should see it listed under `/dev/tty.usbmodemXXXX` or `/dev/tty.usbserialXXXX`.

On Linux, when you connect the Arduino board, you should see it listed under `/dev/ttyACMX` or `/dev/ttyUSBX`.

Exploring the IDE and sketches

Assuming your installation ends successfully, double-click on the Arduino application and you should see the following screen:

The Arduino IDE, first run with an empty sketch

There are two important things you need to do now to properly connect and upload your sketches to the Arduino board. First, select your board by navigating to **Tools | Board**. Then select the serial port of the Arduino board by going to **Tools | Serial Port**.

The final verification step is to run a `Hello world` for Arduino, and you can do so by opening the LED blink example sketch at **File | Examples | 1.Basics | Blink**.

Now, simply click on the **Upload** button in the environment. If the upload is successful, the message **Done uploading** will appear in the status bar.

Wait for a few seconds and you will see the **RX** and **TX** LEDs on the board flashing.

If you have any problems, check out the troubleshooting suggestions at `http://arduino.cc/en/Guide/Troubleshooting`.

Congratulations, your Arduino is up-and-running!

The blood meter project

In this project, we will use a temperature sensor to measure the warmth of your skin and then start to turn on (or off) the LEDs indicated by the temperature.

First, we will tinker with our board and prepare the project with components described earlier in the *Other components you will need* section. Then, we will write the sketch to read sensor data and, based on the data of your skin temperature, we will turn LEDs on and off.

Finally, we will feed our JavaFX application with temperature sensor data and show the result with a chart API to indicate the level of your skin temperature.

Tinkering with the circuit

Now, we are going to tinker with our blood meter circuit shown in the following diagram. Start by connecting the jumper wires between Arduino UNO and the breadboard. I have attached the TMP36 temperature sensor on the breadboard, so the rounded part of the sensor faces away from Arduino. The order of the pins is very important! Note that we have connected the left pin to the power, the right one is grounded, and the center pin that gives the voltage output is connected to the analog pin A0 on the board. The screenshot as follows:

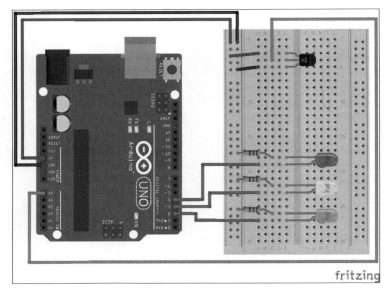

Circuit layout for Blood Meter example

Finally, I have attached the three LED lights and the resistors, and connected them with Arduino pins 4, ~3, and 2 of the digital PMW~ pins row.

As usual, I have connected the breadboard + row to power (5V) and - row to the ground (GND).

 Remember to keep the board unplugged while you set up your components.

The sketch

After we have tinkered with our circuit and have configured everything, we need to program our microcontroller. This is where the sketch will do its magic:

```
/*
  Chapter 7 example
  Project  - Blood-Meter

  This sketch is written to accompany Project in the
  JavaFX 8 essentials book

  Parts required:
  1 TMP36 temperature sensor
  3 red LEDs
  3 220 ohm resistors

  Created 5 April 2015
  by Mohamed Mahmoud Taman
  */

// named constant for the pin the sensor is connected to
const int sensorPin = A0;
// Room temperature in Celsius
const float baselineTemp = 25.0;

void setup() {
  // open a serial connection to display values
  Serial.begin(9600);
  // set the LED pins as outputs
```

```
    // the for() loop saves some extra coding
    for (int pinNumber = 2; pinNumber < 5; pinNumber++) {
      pinMode(pinNumber, OUTPUT);
      digitalWrite(pinNumber, LOW);
    }
}

void loop() {
  // read the value on AnalogIn pin 0
  // and store it in a variable
  int sensorVal = analogRead(sensorPin);

  // send the 10-bit sensor value out the serial port
  Serial.print("Sensor Value: ");
  Serial.print(sensorVal);

  // convert the ADC reading to voltage
  float voltage = (sensorVal / 1024.0) * 5.0;

  // Send the voltage level out the Serial port
  Serial.print(", Volts: ");
  Serial.print(voltage);

  // convert the voltage to temperature in degrees C
  // the sensor changes 10 mV per degree
  // the datasheet says there's a 500 mV offset
  // ((voltage - 500mV) times 100)
  Serial.print(", degrees C: ");
  float temperature = (voltage - .5) * 100;
  Serial.println(temperature);

  // if the current temperature is lower than the baseline
  // turn off all LEDs
  if (temperature < baselineTemp) {
    digitalWrite(2, LOW);
    digitalWrite(3, LOW);
    digitalWrite(4, LOW);
  } // if the temperature rises 2-4 degrees, turn an LED on
  else if (temperature >= baselineTemp + 2 && temperature <
baselineTemp + 4) {
```

```
    digitalWrite(2, HIGH);
    digitalWrite(3, LOW);
    digitalWrite(4, LOW);
  } // if the temperature rises 4-6 degrees, turn a second LED on
  else if (temperature >= baselineTemp + 4 && temperature <
baselineTemp + 6) {
    digitalWrite(2, HIGH);
    digitalWrite(3, HIGH);
    digitalWrite(4, LOW);
  } // if the temperature rises more than 6 degrees, turn all LEDs on
  else if (temperature >= baselineTemp + 6) {
    digitalWrite(2, HIGH);
    digitalWrite(3, HIGH);
    digitalWrite(4, HIGH);
  }
  delay(100);
}
```

How it works

If you are reading the comments of each line, you will understand the code. Without going into the details, the following are the main points of the sketch.

Every Arduino sketch has two main primary methods: setup() and loop(). The first method is for initialization of the pins as input or output, opening the serial ports, setting their speed, and so on. The second method executes the task repeatedly inside the microcontroller.

At the beginning, we have a pair of useful constants: one references analog input and the other holds the baseline temperature. For every 2 *degrees* above this baseline, a LED will turn on.

Inside the setup() method, we initialize the serial port to the desired speed of 9,600 bits per second, and we use a for loop to set some pins as directions (output pins) and turn them off.

Inside the loop() method, we start reading the temperature sensor as voltage values between 0 and 1,023, then send the sensor values to the serial port using Serial. print() so that any connected device (for example, our computer) can read them. These analog readings measure the temperature of the room or of your skin if you touch the sensor.

We need to convert the analog sensor readings into voltage values using the following equation:

```
voltage = (sensorVal / 1024.0) * 5.0
```

From the datasheet, we use the sensor specifications to convert the voltage into temperature using this equation:

```
temperature = (voltage - .5) * 100
```

With the real temperature, you can set up an `if else` statement to light the LEDs. Using the baseline temperature as a starting point, you will turn on one LED for every 2 degrees of temperature increase above that baseline.

You are going to look for a range of values as you move through the temperature scale.

The **Analog-to-Digital Converter (ADC)** reads really fast (in terms of microseconds), and a delay of 1 ms at the end of the `loop()` function is advised. But given that this is going to be sent to the serial port, a 100 ms delay is finally set.

Testing, verifying, and uploading the sketch into the Arduino

With the code uploaded to the Arduino, click on the serial monitor icon as illustrated in the following screenshot:

Arduino IDE toolbar icons

You should see a stream of values coming out, formatted like this:

```
Sensor Value: 158, Volts: 0.77, degrees C: 27.15
```

Now try touching your finger around the sensor while it is plugged into the breadboard and see what happens to the values in the serial monitor.

Make a note of the temperature when the sensor is left in the open air. Close the serial monitor and change the `baselineTemp` constant to what you have observed earlier. Upload the code again and try holding the sensor again; as the temperature increases, you should see LEDs turn on one by one.

Congratulations, hot stuff!

Reading data from serial ports

There is no standard way to read serial ports in Java, as it is a hardware-specific task that breaks the Java multiplatform concept. So, we need a third party library to do the job and it should be written in Java for integration with our application.

Arduino IDE used the first library for serial communication, called **RXTX**. Originally from Trent Jarvi and distributed under LGPL v2.1+ Linking Over Controlled Interface license, it was distributed with Arduino IDE until the 1.5.5 beta version to communicate with the board. However, it was very slow and it is now deprecated.

The new **Java Simple Serial Connector** (**jSSC**) library is developed by Alexey Sokolov and licensed under GNU Lesser GPL. Since the 1.5.6 beta version, the Arduino IDE uses the new library for board communication, as it is faster than its predecessor.

Another big advantage of this library is that it is distributed as a single `jssc.jar` file, which includes all the native interfaces for all platforms to reduce the pain of local installation for each platform and operating system. It adds them to the `classpath` at runtime, as shown in the following screenshot:

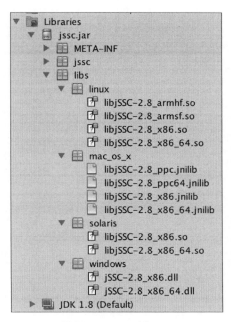

jSSC 2.8.0 native libraries

You can download the latest version from `https://github.com/scream3r/java-simple-serial-connector/releases`. At the time of writing, the jSSC version is 2.8.0.

The JavaFX blood meter monitoring application

We will design a JavaFX 8 application that takes the readings from the temperature sensor and displays the values in a line chart. We will also show what happens to the LEDs on the board with a set of a shapes simulating board LEDs. For the sake of clarity, we'll use two classes one for the serial readings and one for the JavaFX UI and main application BloodMeterFX file, including chart APIs.

We'll bind these classes (Serial and BloodMeterFX) using a StringProperty containing the last line read from the serial port. By listening to changes in this property in the JavaFX thread, we'll know when there's a new reading to add to the chart.

The full project code can be downloaded from the *Packt Publishing* website.

Serial communication in Java

Let's first begin by explaining the Serial.java class. This class code is mostly taken from *JavaFX 8 Introduction By Example, Apress*, with changes in the core reading function, as shown in the following code snippets:

You should include the jSSC.jar file into your classpath, either by adding it to <JAVA_HOME>/jre/lib/ext on Linux or Windows (or /Library/Java/Extensions on the Mac), or preferably by adding it to your project libraries, as in the previous screenshot, if you intended to distribute your application.

In order to be able to read the serial port, we need the following imported jSSC classes:

```
import jssc.SerialPort;
import static jssc.SerialPort.*;
import jssc.SerialPortException;
import jssc.SerialPortList;
```

For dynamically reading the port, if you don't know the exact port name to set through the constructor of this class we have a set of port names to help you select the proper port that the Arduino board can be connected to.

```
private static final List<String> USUAL_PORTS = Arrays.asList(
  "/dev/tty.usbmodem", "/dev/tty.usbserial", //Mac OS X
  "/dev/usbdev", "/dev/ttyUSB", "/dev/ttyACM", "/dev/serial", //Linux
  "COM3", "COM4", "COM5", "COM6" //Windows
);

private final String ardPort;
```

```
public Serial() {
    ardPort = "";
}

public Serial(String port) {
    ardPort = port;
}
```

The `connect()` method looks for a valid serial port if it is not set with an Arduino board connected to it. If it is found, it's opened and a listener is added. This listener is responsible for getting the input readings from the serial port every time a line is returned from the Arduino output. The `stringProperty` is set with that line. We used a `StringBuilder` to store the chars and extract the line content whenever `'\r\n'` is found. We have used bulk operations over collections provided by lambda expressions here to make it simple to look up the port list and return the valid port, depending on the operating system.

Every line found is set to the `line` variable through the `set()` method in order to make the necessary changes to the chart via a registered change listener event to `line` variable, which is exposed through the `getLine()` method. The code is as follows:

```
public boolean connect() {
  out.println("Serial port is openning now...");
  Arrays.asList(SerialPortList.getPortNames()).stream()
  .filter(name -> ((!ardPort.isEmpty() && name.equals(ardPort))
      || (ardPort.isEmpty() && USUAL_PORTS.stream()
  .anyMatch(p -> name.startsWith(p)))))
  .findFirst()
  .ifPresent(name -> {
  try {
    serPort = new SerialPort(name);
      out.println("Connecting to " + serPort.getPortName());
      if (serPort.openPort()) {
        serPort.setParams(BAUDRATE_9600,
        DATABITS_8,
        STOPBITS_1,
        PARITY_NONE);
        serPort.setEventsMask(MASK_RXCHAR);
        serPort.addEventListener(event -> {
          if (event.isRXCHAR()) {
            try {
              sb.append(serPort.readString(event.getEventValue()));
```

```
                      String ch = sb.toString();
                      if (ch.endsWith("\r\n")) {
                        line.set(ch.substring(0, ch.indexOf("\r\n")));
                        sb = new StringBuilder();
                      }
                    } catch (SerialPortException e) {
                      out.println("SerialEvent error:" + e.toString());
                    }
                  }
                });
            }
          } catch (SerialPortException ex) {
            out.println("ERROR: Port '" + name + "': " + ex.toString());
          }});
          return serPort != null;
        }
```

Finally, the disconnect() method is responsible for removing a listener from the port and closing the port connection to free up resources used by the application. The code is as follows:

```
        public void disconnect() {
          if (serPort != null) {
            try {
              serPort.removeEventListener();
              if (serPort.isOpened()) {
                serPort.closePort();
              }
            } catch (SerialPortException ex) {
            out.println("ERROR closing port exception: " +
              ex.toString());
          }
          out.println("Disconnecting: comm port closed.");
        }
      }
```

Application logic and charting API

The main component of our application is the LineChart< Number, Number> chart class API, which will be used to plot your blood temperature level on the Y-axis versus time on the X-axis.

Charts with two axes (such as line, bar, and area charts) have been available since JavaFX 2, and they are of type Node class, which makes it easy to add them to Scene like any other nodes.

In our application, we will add the following createBloodChart() method, which is responsible for creating and preparing the chart and returning it to be added to the main application scene.

At the beginning of the application, we have instance variables: a Serial object to handle Arduino connectivity and readings; listener to be registered with the Serial line object; BooleanProperty to keep track of the connection status; and three float properties that keep track of all sensor data its actual value, its voltage conversion, and finally the voltage converted to temperature in degree Celsius, respectively. The code is as follows:

```
private final Serial serial = new Serial();
private ChangeListener<String> listener;
private final BooleanProperty connection = new
  SimpleBooleanProperty(false);
private final FloatProperty bloodTemp = new
  SimpleFloatProperty(0);
private final FloatProperty volts = new SimpleFloatProperty(0);
private final FloatProperty sensorVal = new
  SimpleFloatProperty(0);
```

We'll add LineChart to plot the temperature level from the temperature sensor, with one Series that take pairs of numbers to be plotted against each axis; these are NumberAxis instances. XYChart.Data is added to the series data as a pair of *X* and *Y* values for every point to plot the readings.

Whenever the size of Series is greater than 40 points, the first values will be removed for memory efficiency. The code is as follows:

```
private LineChart<Number, Number> createBloodChart() {
  final NumberAxis xAxis = new NumberAxis();
  xAxis.setLabel("Temperature Time");
  xAxis.setAutoRanging(true);
  xAxis.setForceZeroInRange(false);
  xAxis.setTickLabelFormatter(new StringConverter<Number>() {
    @Override
    public String toString(Number t) {
      return new SimpleDateFormat("HH:mm:ss").format(new
        Date(t.longValue()));
    }
```

```
    @Override
    public Number fromString(String string) {
      throw new UnsupportedOperationException("Not supported
        yet.");
    }
  });
  final NumberAxis yAxis = new NumberAxis("Temperature value",
    baselineTemp - 10, 40.0, 10);
  final LineChart<Number, Number> bc = new LineChart<>(xAxis,
    yAxis);
  bc.setTitle("Blood temperature vs time");
  bc.setLegendVisible(false);

  Series series = new Series();
  series.getData().add(new Data(currentTimeMillis(),
    baselineTemp));
  bc.getData().add(series);

  listener = (ov, t, t1) -> {
    runLater(() -> {
      String[] values = t1.split(",");
      if (values.length == 3) {
        sensorVal.set(parseFloat(values[0].split(":")[1].trim()));
        volts.set(parseFloat(values[1].split(":")[1].trim()));
        bloodTemp.set(parseFloat(values[2].split(":")[1].trim()));
        series.getData().add(new Data(currentTimeMillis(),
        bloodTemp.getValue()));

        if (series.getData().size() > 40) {
          series.getData().remove(0);
        }
      }

    });
  };
  serial.getLine().addListener(listener);

  return bc;
}
```

The most interesting part here is the change listener `listener = (ov, t, t1) -> {}` we have created using lambda expressions, which will be registered to the `Serial` class `line` object we have described earlier. By doing so, we are able to change chart data once any input from Arduino is detected.

For that, we set the *x* coordinate value as the time when we add the reading in milliseconds (on the chart, it will be formatted as *HH:MM:SS*) and the *y* coordinate value is a float measurement of the level of temperature reported by the Arduino in the String `t1`.

> The main use of `Platform.runLater()` is placing the task of filling the series data with the incoming Arduino input in the JavaFX thread, but also it gives the required time to the `Scene` graph to render the chart, skipping values if they are added too fast.

I have added four shapes of type `Circle`, which will be used to simulate the circuit LEDs on and off based on the temperature level, once any changes are done to `FloatProperty bloodTemp` via the change listener. The code is as follows:

```
Circle IndicatorLevel1 = new Circle(26.0, Color.BLACK);
bloodTemp.addListener((ol, ov, nv) -> {
  tempLbl.setText("Degrees C: ".concat(nv.toString()));

  // if the current temperature is lower than the baseline turn off
all LEDs
  if (nv.floatValue() < baselineTemp +2) {
    IndictorLevel1.setFill(Paint.valueOf("Black"));
    IndictorLevel2.setFill(Paint.valueOf("Black"));
    IndictorLevel3.setFill(Paint.valueOf("Black"));
  } // if the temperature rises 1-3 degrees, turn an LED on
  else if (nv.floatValue() >= baselineTemp + 1 && nv.floatValue()
    < baselineTemp + 3) {
      IndictorLevel1.setFill(Paint.valueOf("RED"));
      IndictorLevel2.setFill(Paint.valueOf("Black"));
      IndictorLevel3.setFill(Paint.valueOf("Black"));
  } // if the temperature rises 3-5 degrees, turn a second LED
    on
  else if (nv.floatValue() >= baselineTemp + 4 &&
    nv.floatValue() < baselineTemp + 6) {
    IndictorLevel1.setFill(Paint.valueOf("RED"));
    IndictorLevel2.setFill(Paint.valueOf("RED"));
```

```
        IndictorLevel3.setFill(Paint.valueOf("Black"));
    }//if the temperature rises more than 6 degrees, turn all LEDs
      on
    else if (nv.floatValue() >= baselineTemp + 6 {
    IndictorLevel1.setFill(Paint.valueOf("RED"));
    IndictorLevel2.setFill(Paint.valueOf("RED"));
    IndictorLevel3.setFill(Paint.valueOf("RED"));
    }
});
```

Finally, the main UI is created by the `loadMainUI()` method, which is responsible for creating the whole UI and binding all the required variables to the UI controls, in order to interact dynamically with the events coming from the Arduino input.

Once the scene root (`BorderPane`) object is prepared and set up by `loadMainUI()`, we create the scene and add it to stage in order to run our application as the following:

```
Scene scene = new Scene(loadMainUI(), 660, 510);
stage.setTitle("Blood Meter v1.0");
stage.setScene(scene);
stage.show();
//Connect to Arduino port and start listening
connectArduino();
```

Finally, the overridden `stop()` method inherited from the `Application` class will take care of any resource freeing by closing the `Serial` ports connection and removing `listener` from line object. The code is as follows:

```
@Override
public void stop() {
  System.out.println("Serial port is closing now...");
  serial.getLine().removeListener(listener);
  if (connection.get()) {
  serial.disconnect();
  connection.set(false);
}}
```

Running the application

With everything in place— the JavaFX project with earlier described classes and the `jssc.jar` library added to it—compile and run your application while your Arduino board is connected to your laptop/PC. If everything is okay, you will see the following screenshot that shows temperature values on the chart against time values, which will be based on your room temperature.

Congratulations, you are now monitoring the Arduino input and you can interact with Arduino through the `jssc.jar` library to control it.

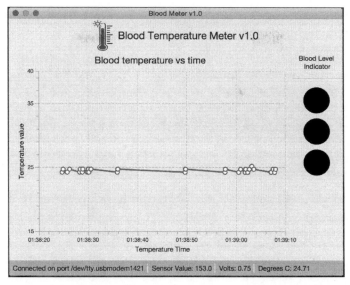

Initial blood meter application readings, with temperature of 24.71 degree

Try to hold the sensor with your fingers and monitor the readings on the chart. In my case, it reached 30.57 degrees. Also, watch the indicator levels on the toolbar and the LEDs on the board. You should see something similar to the following screenshot:

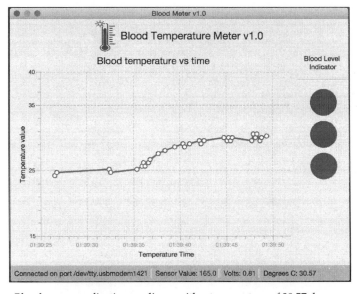

Blood meter application readings, with a temperature of 30.57 degrees

Summary

In this chapter, you learned what can be achieved by combining Arduino and JavaFX. You began by learning about Arduino, its different boards, main specifications, where to buy it and its components. Then, we discussed more sites for projects inspirations.

Next you saw how to download and set up the Arduino IDE to communicate with Arduino. After learning about loading examples in the IDE, you got the chance to try it for yourself by building a simple circuit with an Arduino Uno and a temperature sensor to create a sketch and read the temperature levels in the IDE Serial Monitor.

Then you learned how to read serial port data from your computer using the Java Simple Serial Connector library.

You learned how to use the JavaFX Line Chart API to monitor and display the Arduino readings. Then, you saw an example in which a JavaFX chart is plotted with a series of data from the serial port, using an Arduino board to measure the level of blood temperature with a temperature sensor.

In the next chapter, you will learn about touchless interaction with your computer—without any input devices such as a keyboard, mouse, or even touch devices—using only your hand gestures to control your JavaFX application.

8
Interactive Leap Motion Apps with JavaFX

Now we have come to the most exciting part of the book, where we will dive into the new touchless era of computer-human interaction through body language translated into commands to control surrounding objects and computers.

Every day we notice the rise of input interfaces that are less mouse-centric and more in favor of touchless input. *Gestures* are one of the ways humans can communicate with machines naturally these days.

For decades, motion controls have held a persistent place in our visions of the future. We've watched the super heroes, mad scientists, and space cowboys of popular media control digital experiences with just a wave of their hands.

Tom Cruise does his computing by gesturing

We've been captivated by these powerful, natural, and intuitive interactions — imagining what it would be like to have that power at our own fingertips. For example, *Star Trek's Holodeck* and *Minority Report's pre-crime visioning computers*. Do you remember how Tom Cruise does his computing in the latter using gestures on a transparent display? All exude a sense of power and mastery, along with paradoxical perceptions of simplicity, ease, intuitiveness, and humanity. Simply, these experiences feel magical.

There are several devices on the market that actually allow us to interact with computers using just some parts of our body: many games for the **Xbox**, the Microsoft game console, use the **Kinect** controller to recognize the user's body movements. The myoelectric armband detects movements in your muscles and translates them into gestures so that you can interact with your computer. Leap Motion controller recognizes users' hands and fingers and translate the movements and gestures to the computer.

In this chapter, you will learn about gesture recognition using the **Leap Motion** device, an awesome device that allows a touchless approach to developing enhanced JavaFX applications.

Here are some of the topics that we will discuss in this chapter:

- Introducing the Leap controller, how it works, and where to get one
- Getting and installing the SDK, configuring its driver, and verifying whether it works
- Basics of Leap-based application building blocks
- Developing amazing touchless JavaFX applications

The Leap Motion controller

Here is a very tiny device with 13 mm height, 30 mm width, 76 mm depth, and a weight of 45 grams (*final dimensions: 0.5" x 1.2" x 3"*). With the Leap Motion software running on your computer, just plug the controller into the USB on your Mac or PC and you are ready to go (without any external power source).

Here it works with what it finds above it, capturing the individual movements of your hands and fingers in almost real time (200-300 fps) and translating the gestures into different actions on the application running on your computer. Launched in 2013, this $79.99 device is called the Leap Motion controller.

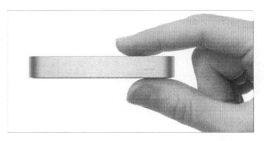

Leap Motion size compared to human hand

From the developer's point of view, this device allows designing applications that can be controlled simply by gestures and movements of the user's *hands* and *fingers*, just like in *Minority Report*!

It senses how you naturally move your hands and lets you use your computer in a whole new way — point, wave, reach, grab, or pick something up and move it. You can do things you never dreamed possible.

Check your hand; just one hand has 29 bones, 29 joints, 123 ligaments, 48 nerves, and 30 arteries. That's sophisticated and complicated. The controller has come really close to figuring it all out.

Actually, when you think about it, the magic of Leap Motion comes in the software, but the company works hard on the hardware to deliver their technology. It has been in development since they started in 2011. The evolution is shown in the following figure:

The evolution of the Leap Motion controller

How it works

Leap Motion's technology, which relies on special receiver hardware and custom software, can track movements to 1/100th millimeter with no visible lag time. The Leap Motion controller has a *150-degree* field of view, and it tracks individual hands and all 10 fingers at 290 fps.

The main hardware of the device consists of three infrared LEDs combined with two monochromatic infrared (IR) cameras. While the LEDs generate a 3D pattern of dots of IR light, the cameras scan the reflected data at nearly 290 fps. Everything within a radius of 50 cm will be scanned and processed, with a resolution of 0.01 mm. The main components of the device are shown in the following figure:

Leap Motion Controller Hardware layers and internal components

This is the future of computer interaction Leap Motion's incredibly fast and accurate natural user interface, which sends all movement data to the computer in a very precise way. The data will be analyzed in the host computer by the Leap Motion proprietary software detection algorithm, and any Leap-enabled application can be interfaced directly without using any other physical input device.

The coordinate system

Mapping the coordinate values received from the controller to the appropriate JavaFX coordinate system is a fundamental task when using the Leap Motion controller in your application.

From the previous discussion, you can observe that the device can detect hands, fingers, and reflective tools within a super-wide 150-degree field of view and a z-axis for depth. This means you can move your hands in 3D, just like you do in the real world.

The device coordinate system uses a right-handed Cartesian coordinate system, with the origin at the center of the device. This is shown in the following figure:

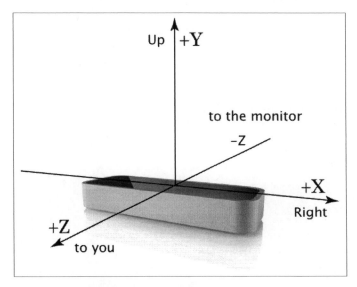

Coordinate system centered in the device

Every time the device scans and analyzes your hand movement into data, a Frame object containing a list of all the processed and tracked data in terms of instances (hands, fingers, and tools) is generated, including a set of motion gestures found in the frame (*swipe, tap, or circle*).

As you may have noticed, the y-axis positive direction is the opposite of the downward orientation in most computer graphics systems, including JavaFX.

However, the fact that the data is referred to the device position and not to the screen, as we are accustomed to with mouse and touch events, changes dramatically the way we need to think.

Fortunately, the API provides several useful methods to find where our hands and fingers are pointing at any time.

Getting the device

As we have been inspired by this amazing technology, we need to engage and start developing something with the device. So, we need to get one first.

The device is available from many vendors such as Amazon, Best buy, and others. However, you can also buy it from the Leap Motion store (`http://store-world. leapmotion.com`).

I bought my device at the end of 2014, and it is possible that you can find special discounts in some of the stores now.

Package contents

When you buy the Leap Motion package, it should contain at least the items shown in the following image:

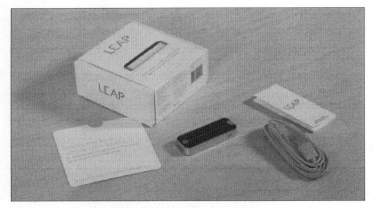

Leap Motion package contents

At the time of writing, the package includes:

- Leap Motion controller
- Two custom-length USB 2.0 cables
- Welcome card
- Important information guide

Getting started with the Leap SDK

Now that we have the hardware, we need to install the software and start development. This is a very easy task; just point your mouse to the address bar of your favorite browser, type the URL https://developer.leapmotion.com/ downloads, and click on the *Enter* key.

At the time of writing, the latest version is SDK 2.2.6.29154. Click on your operating system icon to start downloading the supported version. Alternatively, just click on the green button with the label **Download SDK 2.2.6.29154 for OSX** (for Mac OS X). This will detect your PC/laptop OS and allow you to download the suitable SDK for your OS.

Installing the controller driver and software

The installation process and getting your device ready for interaction require a few simple steps. After downloading the zip content, extract it, install the software installer, and everything should be in place:

1. Download, extract, and run the software installer.

2. After installation, connect your Leap Motion controller and open the Visualizer, as shown in the following screenshot:

Running the Visualizer

3. The SDK consists of a LeapJava.jar libraries and a bunch of native libraries for controller integration. One easy way to integrate LeapJava.jar on your system is by adding the JAR to <JAVA_HOME>/jre/lib/ext on Linux or Windows (or /Library/Java/Extensions on the Mac).

4. Copy the native libraries (`LeapJava.dll`, `Leap.dll`, and `Leapd.dll` for Windows; `libLeapJava.dylib` and `libLeap.dylib` for the Mac; and `libLeapJava.so` and `libLeap.so` for Linux) to the `<JAVA_HOME>/jre/bin` folder.

5. Alternatively, you can just add the JAR to every project as a dependency and load the native libraries as a VM argument `-Djava.library.path=<native library path>`.

The SDK also includes many examples based on supported languages, including the `HelloWorld.java` example, which is a very good base from which to start understanding how to integrate your controller with your Java application.

Verifying whether it works

If everything is okay, a small Leap Motion icon should appear on the taskbar notification area (Windows) or menu bar (Mac), and it should be green as shown in the previous screenshot. The LED indicator on the device should be lit with a green light and *facing you for the correct orientation of the device*.

If you are able to interact and see the visualization of your fingers and hands when the visualizer opens, as shown in the following screenshot, then it is time to start development.

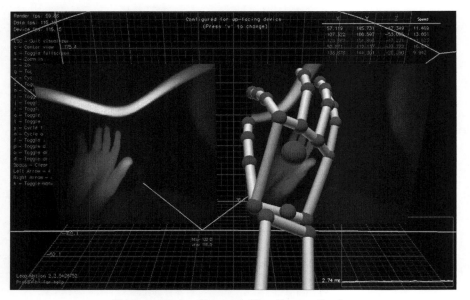

The Leap Motion Diagnostic Visualizer application

Supported languages

Before we deep dive into our application, I would like to just mention that the Leap Motion SDK supports many languages, including Java and others such as JavaScript for Web, C#, C++, Python, Unity, Objective-C, and the Unreal gaming engine.

The Leap JavaFX application

Like you, I can't wait to start the development process, and now you will learn how to interact touchlessly with a JavaFX 8 3D-based application connected to a Leap motion device.

Given that the 3D API has not so far been covered in this book, this is good opportunity to briefly describe the 3D API and bring Leap Motion v2 skeletal modeling (hand in 3D) with some 3D interaction into our JavaFX application.

The Leap Motion API v2.0 introduces a new skeletal tracking model that provides additional information about hands and fingers, predicts the positions of fingers and hands that are not clearly in view, and also improves overall tracking data. For more information on the API, visit https://developer.leapmotion.com/documentation/java/devguide/Intro_Skeleton_API.html?proglang=java.

We are going to build and show how the new skeletal model from Leap Motion v2 can be easily integrated into a JavaFX 3D scene. We will use the predefined 3D shapes API provided by JavaFX to quickly create 3D objects out of the box. These shapes include boxes, cylinders, and spheres that we will use in our application.

The JavaFX 3D API at a glance

3D means *three-dimensional* or something that has *width*, *height*, and *depth* (or *length*). Our physical environment is three-dimensional and we move around in 3D every day.

The JavaFX 3D Graphics library includes Shape3D API, and there are two types of 3D shapes in JavaFX:

- **Predefined shapes**: These are provided to make it easier for you to quickly create 3D objects out-of-the-box. These shapes include boxes, cylinders, and spheres.
- **User-defined shapes**: The JavaFX Mesh class hierarchy contains the TriangleMesh subclass. The Triangle mesh is the most typical kind of mesh used in 3D layouts.

In our application, we are going to use the predefined shapes. For more information about the JavaFX 3D API and examples, please visit `http://docs.oracle.com/javase/8/javafx/graphics-tutorial/javafx-3d-graphics.htm`.

More learning resources

One of the rich resources that will help you in the development and integration process between the Leap Motion controller and your normal Java application is the `HelloWorld.java` example bundled with the SDK.

Another resource that discusses integration with Java is the *Getting Started with Java Development* section from Leap motion documentation, and it is available at `https://developer.leapmotion.com/documentation/java/devguide/Leap_Guides.html`.

The basic application structure

After taking a look inside the `HelloWorld.java` example and the documentation example, you will notice the following points:

- We need a `Controller` object, allowing the connection between the Leap device and the application.
- We need a `Listener` subclass to handle events from the controller.
- Gesture tracking is enabled in the `onConnect()` method.
- The main method in this class is `onFrame()`, a `callback` method dispatched when a new `Frame` object with motion tracking data is available. This object contains list of hands, fingers, or tools and several vectors with their position, orientation, and velocity of movement.
- If gestures are enabled, we'll also get a list of the gestures found, based on the analysis of the last frames. In addition, you will know the status of the gesture whether it has just begun, is in progress, or has ended.

The JavaFX 8 3D application

The application we are going to discuss here is a complex JavaFX 8 3D application that will help you understand the Leap-based application development structure, interact with the device to recognize *hand positions*, and interact with *gestures* to model our hand in a 3D environment.

You can find more resources, including more advanced concepts for developing Leap-based applications with JavaFX, in the examples section later on.

In this application, we are going to detect bones, arms, and joints (position and directions) in the form of cylinder and sphere shapes to model our hands in 3D into our JavaFX application SubScene. Then, we will detect their position to model our real hand movement above the Leap Motion device.

We will also add the raw image so that you can see the model and your real hand in the application's background.

The application consists of three classes:

- LeapListener.java: This class is the listener that interacts with the Leap Motion controller thread to transfer all the analyzed data (arms, bones, fingers, and joints) to the JavaFX application.

- LeapJavaFX.java: This class is a JavaFX application thread that will interact with LeapListener.java in order to create 3D shapes (on every frame), without keeping track of previous ones. Thanks to the power of Observable JavaFX bean properties, which allows data transferred from the Leap thread to be rendered into the JavaFX thread.

- Pair.java: This is a small pair convenience class to store the two bones linked in every joint.

So, let's start and see how we can do this.

You have to enable images on the Leap Motion control panel by checking the **Allow Images** option under the **General** tab, and make sure you disable the **Robust Mode** option for higher image under the **Tracking** tab.

How it works

First, we will explain the main bridge to our application, which is the Leap event listener LeapListener.java.

The main concern when developing a JavaFX application is how to mix the JavaFX thread with other non-JavaFX threads, which in our case is the Leap Motion Event Listener subclass that handles events at a very high rate.

In order to bring these events to a JavaFX thread, we will use the BooleanProperty objects in the LeapListener.java class. Since we will be listening to changes only in doneList object, we don't need the lists to be observable too, because they will be triggering events with any change (adding one bone).

That is why they are plain lists and we use only one Boolean observable property to set it to true after creating all the lists in every Leap `Frame` object:

```
private final BooleanProperty doneList= new
SimpleBooleanProperty(false);
private final List<Bone> bones=new ArrayList<>();
private final List<Arm> arms=new ArrayList<>();
private final List<Pair> joints=new ArrayList<>();
private final List<WritableImage> raw =new ArrayList<>();
```

To get the raw images we have to set this policy `onInit()` and, due to privacy reasons, the user must also enable the feature in the Leap Motion control panel for any application to get the raw camera images.

```
@Override
public void onInit(Controller controller){
  controller.setPolicy(Controller.PolicyFlag.POLICY_IMAGES);
}
```

(As you know, if you want to process gestures, here is where you enable this feature, so maybe you can keep them commented.)

Let's go ahead with creating the Frame method:

```
@Override
public void onFrame(Controller controller) {
  Frame frame = controller.frame();
  doneList.set(false);
  doneList.set(!bones.isEmpty() || !arms.isEmpty());
}
public BooleanProperty doneListProperty() {
  return doneList;
}
```

For every frame, reset `doneList`, process the data, and finally set it to `true` if we have bones or arms (if no hand is over the Leap, the frames are still being processed). Expose the property to be listened on the JavaFX app.

Now processing the frame object data. First, images (this could be done at the end). Clear the list on every frame and then retrieve the images (from the left and right cameras). The Leap documentation is really helpful if you want to understand how this works. Visit `https://developer.leapmotion.com/documentation/java/devguide/Leap_Images.html`.

In fact, this code is part of the first example, adding `PixelWriter` to generate a JavaFX image. Since Leap gives bright pixels, I've negated them *(1- (r|g|b))* to get a negative image, more visible on the hands. Also, I flipped the image from left to right as the following:

```
(newPixels[i*width+(width-j-1)]).raw.clear();
ImageList images = frame.images();
for(Image image : images){
  int width = (int)image.width();
  int height = (int)image.height();
  int[] newPixels = new int[width * height];
  WritablePixelFormat<IntBuffer> pixelFormat =
    PixelFormat.getIntArgbPreInstance();
  WritableImage wi=new WritableImage(width, height);
  PixelWriter pw = wi.getPixelWriter();
  //Get byte array containing the image data from Image object
  byte[] imageData = image.data();

  //Copy image data into display object
  for(int i = 0; i < height; i++){
  for(int j = 0; j < width; j++){
    //convert to unsigned and shift into place
    int r = (imageData[i*width+j] & 0xFF) << 16;
    int g = (imageData[i*width+j] & 0xFF) << 8;
    int b = imageData[i*width+j] & 0xFF;
    // reverse image
    newPixels[i*width+(width-j-1)] = 1- (r | g | b);
  }
  }
  pw.setPixels(0, 0, width, height, pixelFormat, newPixels, 0,
  width);
  raw.add(wi);
}
```

Then clear the bone, arms, and joint lists, as shown in the following code:

```
bones.clear();
arms.clear();
joints.clear();
if (!frame.hands().isEmpty()) {
Screen screen = controller.locatedScreens().get(0);
if (screen != null && screen.isValid()){
```

Get the list of bones; for every finger found, iterate over the types of bones of this finger (up to 5) to avoid the metacarpals of the ring and middle fingers. The code is as follows:

```
for(Finger finger : frame.fingers()){
  if(finger.isValid()){
  for(Bone.Type b : Bone.Type.values()) {
    if((!finger.type().equals(Finger.Type.TYPE_RING) &&
      !finger.type().equals(Finger.Type.TYPE_MIDDLE)) ||
        !b.equals(Bone.Type.TYPE_METACARPAL)){
          bones.add(finger.bone(b));
        }
      }
    }
  }
```

Now we will iterate over the hands list to get each hand arm and add it to the arms list as the following:

```
for(Hand h: frame.hands()){
  if(h.isValid()){
  // arm
  arms.add(h.arm());
```

Now getting the fingers joints. It's a little bit complex to explain in detail how to get every joint. Basically, I find the fingers of every hand, identifying the four fingers other than the thumb. The code is as follows:

```
FingerList fingers = h.fingers();
Finger index=null, middle=null, ring=null, pinky=null;
for(Finger f: fingers){
  if(f.isFinger() && f.isValid()){
    switch(f.type()){
    case TYPE_INDEX: index=f; break;
    case TYPE_MIDDLE: middle=f; break;
    case TYPE_RING: ring=f; break;
    case TYPE_PINKY: pinky=f; break;
    }
  }
}
```

Once I have identified the fingers, I just define the joints between every pair of them (the first three joints) and a joint for the wrist (the last one). The code is as follows:

```
// joints
if(index!=null && middle!=null){
  Pair p=new
    Pair(index.bone(Bone.Type.TYPE_METACARPAL).nextJoint(),
      middle.bone(Bone.Type.TYPE_METACARPAL).nextJoint());
  joints.add(p);
  }
  if(middle!=null && ring!=null){
    Pair p=new
    Pair(middle.bone(Bone.Type.TYPE_METACARPAL).nextJoint(),
    ring.bone(Bone.Type.TYPE_METACARPAL).nextJoint());
    joints.add(p);
  }
  if(ring!=null && pinky!=null){
    Pair p=new
    Pair(ring.bone(Bone.Type.TYPE_METACARPAL).nextJoint(),
    pinky.bone(Bone.Type.TYPE_METACARPAL).nextJoint());
    joints.add(p);
  }
  if(index!=null && pinky!=null){
    Pair p=new Pair(index.bone(Bone.Type.TYPE_METACARPAL).
      prevJoint(),pinky.bone(Bone.Type.TYPE_METACARPAL).
        prevJoint());
    joints.add(p);
  }
```

Finally, the preceding code returns a fresh copy of the bones collection to avoid concurrent exceptions iterating this list. Note that the Leap frame rate is really high. In a powerful computer, it is nearly 5 - 10 ms. The code is as follows:

```
public List<Bone> getBones(){
  return bones.stream().collect(Collectors.toList());
}
```

This is faster than a JavaFX pulse (60 fps, or approximately 16 ms), so lists can be changed while the bones are rendered. With this *clone* method, we avoid any concurrent problem.

The Listener method for the LeapJavaFX application is as follows:

```
Override
  public void start(Stage primaryStage) {
    listener = new LeapListener();
    controller = new Controller();
    controller.addListener(listener);
```

Initialize the Leap listener class and controller, then add the listener:

```
final PerspectiveCamera camera = new PerspectiveCamera();
camera.setFieldOfView(60);
camera.getTransforms().addAll(new Translate(-320,-480,-100));
final PointLight pointLight = new PointLight(Color.ANTIQUEWHITE);
pointLight.setTranslateZ(-500);
root.getChildren().addAll(pointLight);
```

Create a perspective camera for the 3D `subScene`, translate to the middle, bottom of the screen, and to the user. Also, add some punctual light. The code is as follows:

```
rawView=new ImageView();
rawView.setScaleY(2);
```

Create an `ImageView` for the Leap image, which is 640 x 240 with robust mode off (uncheck the option in the Leap control panel), so we scale it up on Y to get a more visible image. The code is as follows:

```
Group root3D=new Group();
root3D.getChildren().addAll(camera, root);
SubScene subScene = new SubScene(root3D, 640, 480, true,
SceneAntialiasing.BALANCED);
subScene.setCamera(camera);
StackPane pane=new StackPane(rawView,subScene);
Scene scene = new Scene(pane, 640, 480);
```

Create a group with the camera and an inner group with light as the root for the `subScene`. Note that the depth buffer and antialiasing are enabled for better rendering. The camera is also added to the `subScene`.

The main root will be a StackPane: on the back, the ImageView, on the front, the transparent SubScene. The code is as follows:

```
final PhongMaterial materialFinger = new
  PhongMaterial(Color.BURLYWOOD);
final PhongMaterial materialArm = new
  PhongMaterial(Color.CORNSILK);
```

Set the material for fingers and arms, with a diffuse color:

```
listener.doneListProperty().addListener((ov,b,b1)->{
  if(b1){
    ...
  }
});
```

We listen to changes in doneList. Whenever it is true (after every frame!), we process the 3D hand(s) rendering:

```
List<Bone> bones=listener.getBones();
List<Arm> arms=listener.getArms();
List<Pair> joints=listener.getJoints();
List<WritableImage> images=listener.getRawImages();
```

First, get the fresh copy of the bones, arms, and joints collection. Then, if there are valid images in the JavaFX thread, we set the image on the ImageView and remove all the root children except for the light (so we are recreating the hand bones all over again):

```
Platform.runLater(()->{
    if(images.size()>0){
    // left camera
    rawView.setImage(images.get(0));
  }
  if(root.getChildren().size()>1){
    // clean old bones
    root.getChildren().remove(1,root.getChildren().size()-1);
}
```

Bones Iterate over the list and add the bones to the scene. If the collection changes, there won't be any concurrent exceptions when we iterate over its copy.

```
bones.stream().filter(bone -> bone.isValid() && bone.length()>0)
.forEach(bone -> {
```

Now we create a cylinder for every bone. This involves some calculations. If you want to go into detail, take each bone as a vector with a position and a direction. Create a vertical cylinder whose radius is half of the width of the bone and whose height is the same as its length. Then, assign it the material. The code is as follows:

```
final Vector p=bone.center();
// create bone as a vertical cylinder and locate it at its center
position
Cylinder c=new Cylinder(bone.width()/2,bone.length());
c.setMaterial(materialFinger);
```

Then we get the cross product of the real bone direction with the vertical one; this gives us the perpendicular vector of rotation. (Signs are due to changes in the coordinate systems). The ang object is the angle between those two vectors. A transformation can be applied with translation to the center of the bone and a rotation of ang around the given vector. The code is as follows:

```
// translate and rotate the cylinder towards its direction
final Vector v=bone.direction();
Vector cross = (new Vector(v.getX(),-v.getY(),
  v.getZ())).cross(new Vector(0,-1,0));
double ang=(new Vector(v.getX(),-v.getY(),-v.getZ())).angleTo(new
  Vector(0,-1,0));
c.getTransforms().addAll(new Translate(p.getX(),-p.getY(),-
  p.getZ()),new Rotate(-Math.toDegrees(ang), 0, 0, 0, new
    Point3D(cross.getX(),-cross.getY(),cross.getZ())));
  // add bone to scene
root.getChildren().add(c);
```

Now spheres at the beginning and at the end of every bone:

```
// add sphere at the end of the bone
Sphere s=new Sphere(bone.width()/2f);
s.setMaterial(materialFinger);
s.getTransforms().addAll(new Translate(p.getX(),-
  p.getY()+bone.length()/2d,-p.getZ()),new Rotate(-
    Math.toDegrees(ang), 0, -bone.length()/2d, 0, new
      Point3D(cross.getX(),-cross.getY(),cross.getZ())));
  // add sphere to scene
  root.getChildren().add(s);
  // add sphere at the beginning of the bone
  Sphere s2=new Sphere(bone.width()/2f);
  s2.setMaterial(materialFinger);
```

```
    s2.getTransforms().addAll(new Translate(p.getX(),-p.getY()-
    bone.length()/2d,-p.getZ()),new Rotate(Math.toDegrees(ang), 0,
      bone.length()/2d, 0, new Point3D(cross.getX(),-
        cross.getY(),cross.getZ()))));
    // add sphere to scene
    root.getChildren().add(s2);
});
```

Now for the joints; we use cylinders again. The distance between the two elements connected gives the length and we get the position and direction to generate and transform the cylinder. The code is as follows:

```
joints.stream().forEach(joint->{
    double length=joint.getV0().distanceTo(joint.getV1());
    Cylinder c=new Cylinder(bones.get(0).width()/3,length);
    c.setMaterial(materialArm);
    final Vector p=joint.getCenter();
    final Vector v=joint.getDirection();
    Vector cross = (new Vector(v.getX(),-v.getY(),
      v.getZ())).cross(new Vector(0,-1,0));
    double ang = (new Vector(v.getX(),-v.getY(),-
      v.getZ())).angleTo(new Vector(0,-1,0));
    c.getTransforms().addAll(
      new Translate(p.getX(),-p.getY(),-p.getZ()), new Rotate(-
        Math.toDegrees(ang), 0, 0, 0, new Point3D(cross.getX(),-
          cross.getY(),cross.getZ()))));
    // add joint to scene
    root.getChildren().add(c);
});
```

Finally, we take the length from the distance between elbow and wrist. All of this is in the API at: https://developer.leapmotion.com/documentation/java/api/Leap.Arm.html. The code is as follows:

```
arms.stream().
filter(arm->arm.isValid()).
forEach(arm->{
    final Vector p=arm.center();
    // create arm as a cylinder and locate it at its center position
    Cylinder c=new Cylinder(arm.width()/2,arm.elbowPosition().
    minus(arm.wristPosition()).magnitude());
    c.setMaterial(materialArm);
```

```
// rotate the cylinder towards its direction
final Vector v=arm.direction();
Vector cross = (new Vector(v.getX(),-v.getY(),-
  v.getZ())).cross(new Vector(0,-1,0));
double ang=(new Vector(v.getX(),-v.getY(),-v.getZ())).
angleTo(new Vector(0,-1,0));
c.getTransforms().addAll(new Translate(p.getX(),-p.getY(),-
  p.getZ()),new Rotate(- Math.toDegrees(ang), 0, 0, 0,
    new Point3D(cross.getX(),- cross.getY(),cross.getZ())));
// add arm to scene
root.getChildren().add(c);
});
```

Running the application

Congratulations! Now connect your Leap controller (the leap icon should be green) and run your application. If everything is okay, you should initially see an empty application scene, as shown in the following screenshot:

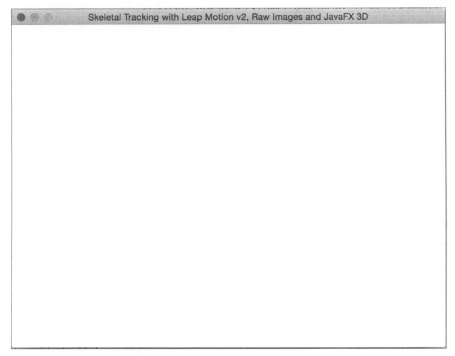

Initial run of the Leap JavaFX application

Move and wave your hand around and the skeletal modeling of your hand should appear with your real hands in the background, responding to your real movements as shown here:

Interaction of Leap JavaFX application and Leap Controller

Try a different arm or hand pattern and position; you should have this replicated in your JavaFX application scene, as shown in the following screenshot:

Interaction of Leap JavaFX application and Leap Controller, with a different hand pattern

More examples

For more examples of using JavaFX with the Leap Motion device, please refer to online resources such as http://www.parleys.com/share.html#play/525467d 6e4b0a43ac12124ad or http://jperedadnr.blogspot.com.es/2013/06/leap-motion-controller-and-javafx-new.html. For interaction with other programming languages, please visit https://developer.leapmotion.com/gallery.

Summary

In this chapter, you learned about the impressive Leap Motion device, and the really nice combination effects that result from using it to enhance JavaFX applications.

You began by learning about the device and how it works. Next, we discussed its SDK for Java and explored a simple application where you learned about listening and processing the data from the Leap device in one thread, while triggering events in the JavaFX thread to deal with them in the scene graph.

In the next chapter, I'll provide advanced tools and resources intended for true JavaFX gurus.

Become a JavaFX Guru

Will your JavaFX 8 journey stop here? Definitely not! JavaFX is a very big topic, which grows day by day, from its core releases from Oracle with new features, functionalities, and stability, to many community individuals and companies that create third-party libraries to fill any missing gaps you may experience, or invent new ones around it, that don't exist in the core.

Of course, with this book, I cannot cover all JavaFX 8 topics. Instead, I tried to scratch the surface of many JavaFX areas, and open topics keys in order to make your adventure easier, by finding your way and getting an idea of how to do it yourself.

However, we also discussed many other tools and technologies, by developing traditional web and desktop applications, and then moved to a more advanced and market demanding area, which is mobile development.

The more we explore the future by learning about **IoT**, which is the next era of information technology, the more we cover interesting topics. We have seen motion many times in movies and have imagined it, and we have made our dreams come true by developing an enhanced touch-less based JavaFX 8 with an amazing Leap Motion v2 gadget.

There is much more to become a JavaFX subject matter and gaining other experiences, which we did not discuss in this book.

So, where do we go from here?

Now, since you have many up and running JavaFX 8 applications, and an understanding of how it works on many platforms and hardware, the rest is up to you and your ingenuity.

Join the community on Facebook, Twitter, and follow the technology expert's blogs, JavaFX blog at `http://blogs.oracle.com/javafx/`, and find news, demos, and insight at `http://fxexperience.com/`. Above all, experiment.

At the end of this chapter, be sure to check out the many *frameworks*, *libraries*, and *projects* that use JavaFX in production today.

Resources and references

In this section, you will find many useful links and references that will help you gain further knowledge about all JavaFX topics.

Official documentation

- **JavaFX documentation**: This is a great resource pointing toward all JavaFX resources, news, experiences, videos, books, API documentation, technical articles, and tutorials:

  `http://www.oracle.com/technetwork/java/javase/documentation/javafx-docs-2159875.html`

- **Java Platform, Standard Edition (Java SE) 8**: These are *Client Technologies*, contains many samples covering all JavaFX topics: `http://docs.oracle.com/javase/8/javase-clienttechnologies.htm`

JavaFX samples

One of the greatest resources to start learning JavaFX 8 is the Java Development Kit 8 samples and demos, which include a JavaFX demo folder that contains many fantastic and advanced applications that cover all JavaFX topics with source code that you can experiment with yourself.

You can download the samples, by just visiting the following link `http://www.oracle.com/technetwork/java/javase/downloads/jdk8-downloads-2133151.html`, and then go to the **Java SE Development Kit 8u45 Demos and Samples Downloads** table, check the **Accept License Agreement** radio button, and click on the zip file link relevant to your operating system, as shown in the following figure:

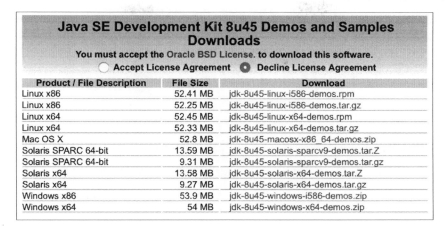

Download JDK & JavaFX 8 demos and samples

The samples zip file contains pre-built samples that you can run, plus the NetBeans project files for each sample.

Extracting the zip file produces the following directory structure:

```
--src    (Contains a NetBeans project for each sample)
 --<Sample1>
 --nbproject
 --src
 --build.xml
 --manifest.mf
 --<Sample2>
 <sample1>.jar (Runs the sample as a standalone application)
<sample2>.jar
```

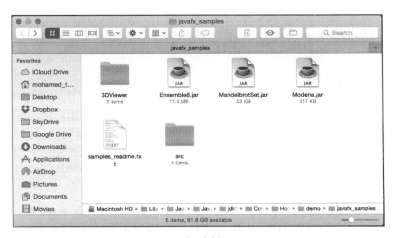

JavaFX samples folder contents

Any `sample.jar` can run as a standalone application; double-click on the JAR file and we have four applications:

1. `Ensemble8.jar`: A gallery of sample applications that demonstrate a large variety of JavaFX features, including animation, charts, and controls. For each sample, you can do the following on all platforms:

   ° View and interact with the running sample

   ° Read its description.

   You can do the following for each sample on desktop platforms only:

   ° Copy its source code

   ° For several samples, you can adjust the properties of the sample components

   ° If you are connected to the Internet, you can also follow links to the relevant API documentation *Ensemble8 also runs with JavaFX for ARM (means running on Raspberry Pi)*.

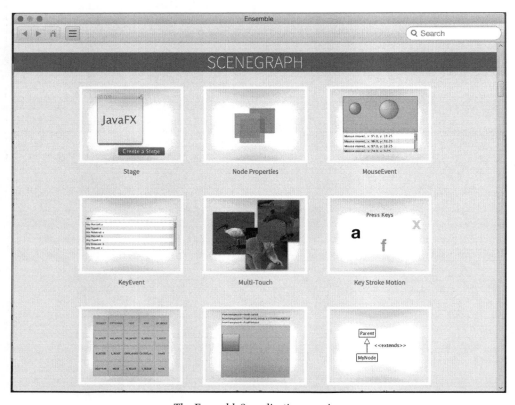

The Ensemble8 application running

2. `MandelbrotSet.jar`: A sample application that demonstrates the advantages of parallel execution done using the Java Parallel API.

    The application renders an image using the Mandelbrot set algorithm and provides intuitive navigation within the range of input parameters.

    More information is available in the `index.html` file inside the `MandelbrotSet` folder.

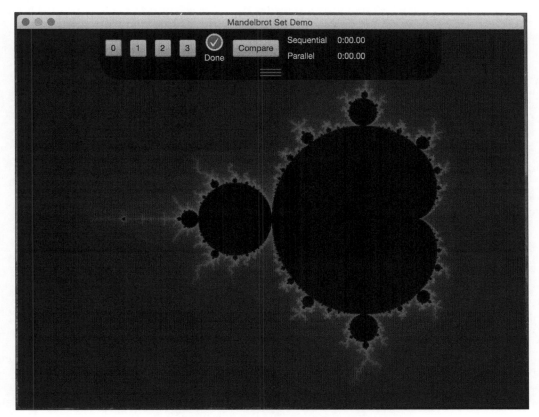

The MandelbrotSet application running

3. `Modena.jar`: A sample application that demonstrates the look and feel of UI components using the `Modena` theme. It gives you the option to contrast the `Modena` and `Caspian` themes and explore various aspects of these themes.

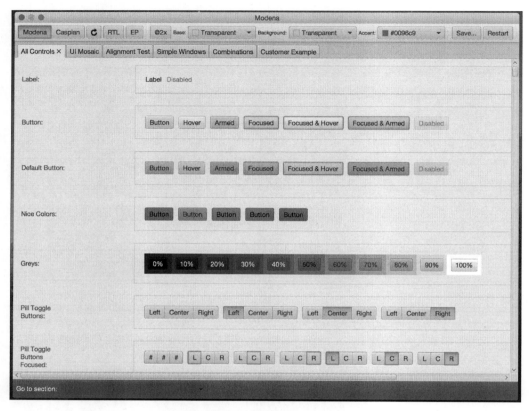

The Modena application running

4. `3DViewer.jar`: 3DViewer is a sample application that allows the user to navigate and examine a 3D scene with a mouse or a track pad. 3DViewer has importers for a subset of the features in **OBJ** and Maya files.

The ability to import animation is also provided for Maya files. (Note that, in the case of Maya files, the construction history should be deleted on all the objects when saving as a Maya file.) 3DViewer also has the ability to export the contents of the scene as Java or FXML files.

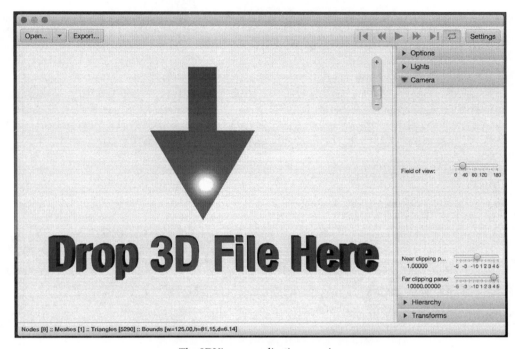

The 3DViewer application running

In order to play with the code yourself and to experiment with any changes you may have, congratulations, you have this chance to do this by running all the previously mentioned applications from **NetBeans** as follows:

5. In the NetBeans IDE, click on **Open Project** in the toolbar, or on the **File** menu and select **Open Project**.

6. Navigate to the location in which you unzipped the samples, and in the `src` directory, select a project and then click on **Open**.

7. To run the application in the NetBeans IDE, in the **Project** pane, right-click on the project and choose **Run**.

Java SE 8

As a reminder, JavaFX 8 is built into the Java 8 SDK. This means that you only need to download the Java 8 SDK. The Java 8 software development kit and related information can be downloaded from the following locations:

- Java 8 at Oracle Technology Network:

  `http://oracle.com/java8`

- The Java development kit:

  `http://www.oracle.com/technetwork/java/javase/downloads/index.html`

- What is new in Java 8? Let's check the new features of Java 8:

  `http://www.oracle.com/technetwork/java/javase/8-whats-new-2157071.html`

- Java SE 8 new features tour:

  `http://tamanmohamed.blogspot.com/2014/06/java-se-8-new-features-tour-big-change.html`

The Java SE 8 API documentation and tutorials

The Java 8 documentation and guides are at the following links:

- The Java SE 8 Javadoc API documentation:

  `http://docs.oracle.com/javase/8`

- The JavaFX 8 Javadoc API documentation:

  `http://docs.oracle.com/javase/8/javafx/api`

- The Java SE 8 Overview Documentation:

  `http://docs.oracle.com/javase/8/docs/index.html`

- The Java SE 8 tutorial:

  `http://docs.oracle.com/javase/tutorial/tutorialLearningPaths.html`

Project Lambda

The core Java SE 8 added language features are lambda expressions and the stream API. The following references are road maps, blogs, and videos of topics surrounding project lambda:

- State of the Lambda, Brian Goetz (Oracle):

  `http://cr.openjdk.java.net/~briangoetz/lambda/lambda-state-final.html`

- Java 8 Revealed: Lambdas, Default Methods and Bulk Data Operations, Anton Arhipov:

  `http://zeroturnaround.com/rebellabs/java-8-revealed-lambdas-defaultmethods-and-bulk-data-operations`

- 10 examples of Lambda Expressions and Streams in Java 8, Javin Paul:

  `http://javarevisited.blogspot.com/2014/02/10-example-of-lambdaexpressions-in-java8.html`

- Java SE 8: Lambda Quick Start, Oracle:

  `http://www.oracle.com/webfolder/technetwork/tutorials/obe/java/Lambda-QuickStart/index.html`

- Java 8: Closures, Lambda Expressions Demystified, Frank Hinkel:

  `http://frankhinkel.blogspot.com/2012/11/java-8-closures-lambdaexpressions.html`

Nashorn

Java SE 8 includes a new scripting engine called **Nashorn**, which is a new and improved JavaScript engine for the Java runtime. The engine enables developers to use the JavaScript language to program applications.

The following links and references are articles and blogs describing Nashorn:

- Oracle's Nashorn: A next Generation JavaScript Engine for the JVM, Julien Ponge:

  `http://www.oraclejavamagazine-digital.com/javamagazine_twitter/20140102/?pg=60#pg60`

- Open JDK's Nashorn site:

  `https://wiki.openjdk.java.net/display/Nashorn/Main`

- The Nashorn blog:

  `https://blogs.oracle.com/Nashorn`

JavaFX properties and bindings

Properties and bindings are essential to JavaFX when synchronizing values between JavaFX nodes.

The following are great resources about read-only properties, listeners, and the role of JavaFX Beans:

- Creating Read-Only Properties in JavaFX, Michael Heinrichs:

  `http://blog.netopyr.com/2012/02/02/creating-read-only-properties-injavafx`

- The Unknown JavaBean, Richard Bair:

  `https://weblogs.java.net/blog/rbair/archive/2006/05/the_unknown_jav.html`

- Using JavaFX Properties and Binding, Scott Hommel:

  `http://docs.oracle.com/javafx/2/binding/jfxpub-binding.htm`

- Pro JavaFX 8, (*Chapter 4, Properties and Bindings*), Johan Vos, James Weaver, Weiqi Gao, Stephen Chin, and Dean Iverson, (Apress, 2014):

  `http://www.apress.com/9781430265740`

- Open Dolphin: A JavaFX MVC framework (founded by Dierk Koenig of Canoo Engineering):

  `http://open-dolphin.org/dolphin_website/Home.html`

- JavaFX MVP framework based on Convention over Configuration and Dependency Injection (founded by Adam Bien):

  `http://afterburner.adam-bien.com`

JavaFX communities

So you want to get involved with the JavaFX community? Please check out the following links:

- The Java.net JavaFX community site:

  `https://www.java.net/community/javafx`

- FXExperience: JavaFX News, Demos and Insight (@fxexperience):

  `http://fxexperience.com`

- Nighthacking (@_nighthacking): Hosted by Stephen Chin. A tour around the world to see everything about Java, JavaFX, and IoT. Amazing live talks.

  `http://nighthacking.com`

- Oracle's JavaFX Community portal to Real World Use Cases, Community Support, Third-Party tools and Open JFX:

  `http://www.oracle.com/technetwork/java/javase/community/index.html`

- JFXtras: A JavaFX custom controls community:

  `http://jfxtras.org`

- ControlsFX: Another custom controls community, started by Jonathan Giles of Oracle:

  `http://fxexperience.com/controlsfx`

- Silicon valley JavaFX users group:

  `http://www.meetup.com/svjugfx`

- Silicon valley JavaFX users group Live stream:

  `http://www.ustream.tv/channel/silicon-valley-javafx-user-group`

- Oracle Forums on JavaFX:

  `https://community.oracle.com/community/developer/english/java/javafx/javafx_2.0_and_later`

Java SE / JavaFX books and magazines

The following links are newer book titles that relate to the new Java SE 8 and JavaFX 8 platform:

- An Amazing book, *JavaFX 8: Introduction by Example, Second Edition*, Carl Dea, Mark Heckler, Gerrit Grunwald, José Pereda, and Sean M. Phillips (Apress, 2014. ISBN: 978-1-4302-6460-6)

  `http://www.apress.com/9781430264606`

- Pro JavaFX 8, Johan Vos, James Weaver, Weiqi Gao, Stephen Chin, and Dean Iverson (Apress, 2014. ISBN: 978-1-4302-6574-0)

  `http://www.apress.com/9781430265740`

- Java 8 Recipes, Josh Juneau (Apress, 2014. ISBN: 978-1-4302-6827-7)

  http://www.apress.com/9781430268277

- JavaFX Rich Client Programming on the NetBeans Platform, Paul Anderson and Gail Anderson (Addison-Wesley Professional, 2014. ISBN: 978-0321927712):

  https://blogs.oracle.com/geertjan/entry/new_book_javafx_rich_client

  http://www.amazon.com/JavaFX-Client-Programming-NetBeans-Platform/dp/0321927710

- Mastering JavaFX 8 Controls, Hendrik Ebbers (Oracle Press, 2014. ISBN: 9780071833776):

  http://mhprofessional.com/product.php?isbn=0071833773

  http://www.guigarage.com/javafx-book

- Quick Start Guide to JavaFX, J.F. DiMarzio (Oracle Press, 2014. ISBN: 978-0071808965):

  http://www.mhprofessional.com/product.php?isbn=0071808965

- Java SE 8 for the Really Impatient, Cay S. Horstmann (Addison-Wesley, 2014. ISBN 978-0321927767)

  http://www.addison-wesley.de/9780321927767.html

- Mastering Lambdas, Maurice Naftalin (Oracle Press, 2014. ISBN: 007-1829628):

  http://www.mhprofessional.com/product.php?isbn=0071829628

- Java Magazine from Oracle:

  http://www.oracle.com/technetwork/java/javamagazine/index.html

I appreciate your time, and I hope you enjoyed reading this book as much as I enjoyed writing it for you. Thank you.

Index

Symbols

A

B

C

Thank you for buying
JavaFX Essentials

About Packt Publishing

Packt, pronounced 'packed', published its first book, *Mastering phpMyAdmin for Effective MySQL Management*, in April 2004, and subsequently continued to specialize in publishing highly focused books on specific technologies and solutions.

Our books and publications share the experiences of your fellow IT professionals in adapting and customizing today's systems, applications, and frameworks. Our solution-based books give you the knowledge and power to customize the software and technologies you're using to get the job done. Packt books are more specific and less general than the IT books you have seen in the past. Our unique business model allows us to bring you more focused information, giving you more of what you need to know, and less of what you don't.

Packt is a modern yet unique publishing company that focuses on producing quality, cutting-edge books for communities of developers, administrators, and newbies alike. For more information, please visit our website at www.packtpub.com.

About Packt Open Source

In 2010, Packt launched two new brands, Packt Open Source and Packt Enterprise, in order to continue its focus on specialization. This book is part of the Packt Open Source brand, home to books published on software built around open source licenses, and offering information to anybody from advanced developers to budding web designers. The Open Source brand also runs Packt's Open Source Royalty Scheme, by which Packt gives a royalty to each open source project about whose software a book is sold.

Writing for Packt

We welcome all inquiries from people who are interested in authoring. Book proposals should be sent to author@packtpub.com. If your book idea is still at an early stage and you would like to discuss it first before writing a formal book proposal, then please contact us; one of our commissioning editors will get in touch with you.

We're not just looking for published authors; if you have strong technical skills but no writing experience, our experienced editors can help you develop a writing career, or simply get some additional reward for your expertise.

Mastering JavaScript Design Patterns

ISBN: 978-1-78398-798-6   Paperback: 290 pages

Discover how to use JavaScript design patterns to create powerful applications with reliable and maintainable code

1. Learn how to use tried and true software design methodologies to enhance your Javascript code.

2. Discover robust JavaScript implementations of classic as well as advanced design patterns.

3. Packed with easy-to-follow examples that can be used to create reusable code and extensible designs.

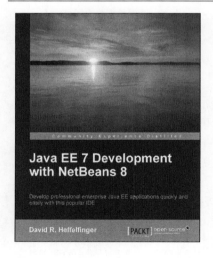

Java EE 7 Development with NetBeans 8

ISBN: 978-1-78398-352-0   Paperback: 364 pages

Develop professional enterprise Java EE applications quickly and easily with this popular IDE

1. Use the features of the popular NetBeans IDE to accelerate your development of Java EE applications.

2. Covers the latest versions of the major Java EE APIs such as JSF 2.2, EJB 3.2, JPA 2.1, CDI 1.1, and JAX-RS 2.0.

3. Walks you through the development of applications utilizing popular JSF component libraries such as PrimeFaces, RichFaces, and ICEfaces.

Please check **www.PacktPub.com** for information on our titles

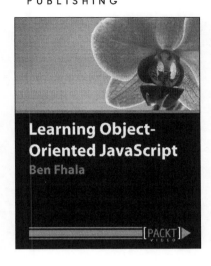

Learning Object-Oriented JavaScript

ISBN: 978-1-78355-433-1   Duration: 02:47 hours

Acquire advanced JavaScript skills and create complex and reusable applications

1. Discover the important concepts of object-oriented programming (OOP) and make your life easier, more enjoyable, and more focused on what you love doing—creating.

2. Develop reusable code while creating three different clocks, a classic clock, a text clock, and an alarm clock.

3. Utilize the advantages of using constructors, methods, and properties to become an expert.

Java EE Development with NetBeans 7

ISBN: 978-1-78216-246-9   Duration: 03:08 hours

Develop professional enterprise Java EE applications by taking advantage of the time-saving features of the NetBeans 7 IDE

1. Use the features of the popular NetBeans IDE along with keyboard shortcuts to accelerate development of Java EE applications.

2. Take advantage of the NetBeans debugger to get rid of bugs that may creep into your Java EE code.

3. Learn about all the major Java EE APIs as well as tips on how to effectively use the NetBeans IDE to save time when developing Java EE applications.

Please check **www.PacktPub.com** for information on our titles